TNTRIO MOVEMENT

BOOK - 7

Franklin Ysaac + Eliseo Rio Jr. + Gus Lagman

June 2023

*Published in USA in June 2023 by
TATAY JOBO ELIZES,
Self-Publisher, under the permission and
authorization of*

*Franklin Ysaac, et al
authors and copyright owners.*

*The copyright owner can withdraw this permission
at his discretion without any objection from Tatay
Jobo Elizes at any time. Printing of this book is
using the present day method of Print-On-Demand
(POD) system, where prints will never run out of
copies to be available for posterity.
The copyright owner is free to republish with other
publishers anytime.*

*KDP ISBN: 9798398427714
Independently Published*

*Contact: job_elizes@yahoo.com +
https://www.facebook.com/franklin.ysaac +
http://tinyurl.com/mj76ccq (amazon site) +
www.tatayjoboelizes.webs.com +
https://www.facebook.com/groups/399368500835109*

Content

....

Preface

The main subject of this book and previous books is about results of the May 9, 2022 national elections in the Philippines.

A team of IT experts composed of the three(3) authors of these books have initiated moves to write about their findings and technical analyses of the election results.

The findings are well explained in many writings and postings in social media, particularly facebook, and the actions taken by them with the support of many sectors of society.

The updates had been recorded in previous books, published at amazondotcom, which are the following titles:

1–Truth Petition to Comelec (Initial book)
2—Truth Warriors-1
3—Initial Stages of Truth Petition
4—Truth Warriors-2
5—Truth Patriots-1
6—Writ of Mandamus Petition
7—TNTrio Movement Book-1
8—TNTrio Movement Book-2
9—TNTrio Movement Book-3
10- TNTRIO Movement Book-4
11–TNTRIO Movement Book-5
12—THTRIO Movement Book-6
13—THTRIO Movement Book-7 (this one)

As this is a continuing movement, more books will be published from collection of writings and postings in the web to record all developments for posterity and guidance of all concerned.

....

1
Politics affecting Election Issues – Odono, Meman, Cleofe Arguments – May 18, 2023

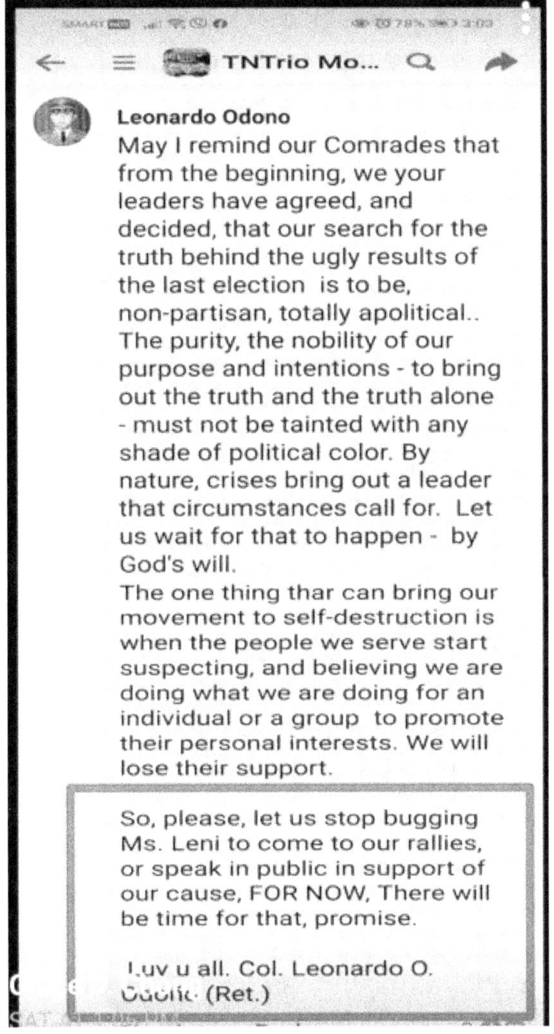

Jacinto   Meman is   at Sierra   Madre   - Philippines".

"sa aking pananaw"

Our search for the TRUTH is for us to be enlightened on what really transpired in the election of May 2022 which the COMELEC must come clean. If they're not complicit to any anomalies in the conduct of the said election why don't they just bring out what the petitioners- the TNTRIO are asking for? Or are they so afraid of what they've done? As Col. Odono said let's not drag personalities into this or the people in government will put a political color into the search for the TRUTH.
K.I.M.#77

....

Donnie Cleofe

Just a question. How can we exclude those who were deceived in a political exercise like the election? Candidates deceived, voters deceived in a widespread fraud of the Comelec syndicate and BBM-Duterte-GMA Triad. This syndicate stepped on democracy and the issue is political. Now you want to give a non political solution. Millions of people who were cheated. Do you want them all to shut up because they sympathize with politicians? Politician or non politician are affected by the erosion of our democracy so everyone has a right to fight and be heard. Will the COMELEC and Supreme Court hear you if you are just fighting? This is not the season for excessive cleaning. We are already being pigged but we still want to act angel. Can we win if that's our style? Real talk only.

Translation in filipino
Donnie Cleofe
Tanong ko lang po. Paano natin iitsa puwera ang mga taong nadaya mismo sa isang political exercise kagaya ng eleksyon? Nadaya ang mga kandidato, nadaya ang mga botante sa isang malawakang pandaraya ng sindikatong Comelec at BBM-Duterte-GMA Triad. Demokrasya ang niyurakan nitong sindikato

at ang isyu ay political. Ngayon gusto nyong bigyan ng non political solusyon. Milyon po ang kakampink na nadaya. Gusto nyo bang manahimik silang lahat dahil sila ay sumisimpatiya sa mga pulitiko? Pulitiko o hindi pulitiko ay apektado sa pagyurak ng demokrssya natin kaya lahat ay may karapatan na lumaban at marinig. Pakinggan kaya kayo ng COMELEC at Supreme Court kung kakarampot kayong lumalaban? Hindi po ito panahon ng sobrang pagpapalinis. Binababoy na tayo gusto pa natin magkilos anghel. Manalo kaya tayo kung ganyan stilo natin? Realtalk lang po.

....

2
Supreme Court Filings soon - Franklin Ysaac – May 18, 2023

nagpatunay na Hindi makatotoo ang buong pangyayaring eleksyon .

Ngayon, sa tulong ng ating abogado,maghain tayo uli ng supplemental sa korte Suprema para mag paliwanag sa iregularidad ang comelec para malaman ng taumbayan ang malaking pag babaliktad ng resulta .

At para Mas mapatunayan na Hindi totoo, maghahain uli ng supplemental petition na ilabas na ng telco ang CDRs na magpapatunay na Meron o walang ganun 20M plus transmisssion nung unang Oras mula Alas Siete hanggang alas otso. Pag walang transmission sa palagay namin, tunay na Yung transmission ay ginawang milagro .

Abangan po natin etong supplemental at malapit na rin tayo sa katotohanan.

Hindi po talaga natutulog ang Diyos at ang kanyang Ina na sumasaklolo parati sa mga hiling at dasal ng buong sambayanan.

Maraming Salamat po O Diyos na matulungin at maawain.

Mahal namin Mama Mary, Maraming Salamat sa pag gabay niyo po sa amin.

Huwag po kayong magsawa na tumulong at mag milagro po sa mga taga sunod po sa utos ng Inyong Anak na si Hesus.

Abangan po namin na Sana matapos na rin ang kalbaryo namin na ngayon isang taon na naghirap at nakaranas ng kahirapan .

Marami pa susunod kami hihilingin sa Inyo po at pag sinagot na mga supplemental petition namin Giginhawa na rin ang pakiramdam ng taumbayan .

Amen .

Last May 9, our novena to San Jose ended!

In front of the Image of Santa Maria de la Immaculada Concepcion in Manila Cathedral, our companions did Rosary and Novena led by Sister Teresita Elevera of Franciscan Sisters of Mary.

Thanks to those who attended the church and as we said the miracle was at the end.

Comelec released something that the election results do not match with the transmission logs. Obviously there is a miracle done in the real result and proved that the whole election event is not true.

Now, with the help of our lawyer, let's file a supplementary file again to the Supreme Court to explain the irregularity of the comelec so that the people will know the big reversal of the results.

And to prove that it is not true, telco will again file a supplemental petition that will prove that there is or does not have that 20M plus transmission in the first hour from seven to eight o'clock. If there is no transmission in our opinion, it is true that the transmission was made a miracle.

Let's wait for this supplemental and we are also close to the truth.

God and His Mother never sleeps who always helps the wishes and prayers of the whole congregation.

Thank you very much, O God who is helpful and merciful.

Our beloved Mama Mary, Thank you very much for guiding us.

Don't get tired of helping and doing miracles to the followers of Your Son Jesus.

Let's wait for the Calvary that has been suffering for a year and experienced hardship will finally end.

More will follow, we will ask from you and when our supplemental petitions are answered, the feeling of the countrymen will be relieved.

Amen .

....

3
Letter to former VP Leni Robredo
May 19, 2023
Hon. Leni Gerona Robredo
Former Vice-President, Philippines
Dear VP Leni,

May 9, 2022, marked a devastating day for many Filipinos when the election results showed that Marcos had overwhelmingly won the presidency.

A young boy and his sister, who had joined their parents in every pink rally in Metro Manila, asked their mother with tears in their eyes, "Why, mom, why? Haven't we worked hard enough for VP Leni? What will happen to us now?"

Sadly, their mother had no answers, as she too was devastated, like millions of other Filipinos, who hoped and dreamed of a better and brighter future for their children. When you declared, as advised by your lawyers, that there was no evidence of fraud in the election, it was the end of hope for many.

All seemed so dark then, until light came through the cracks, in the person of the three wise men who appeared on the scene, known as the TNTrio, standing for Truth and Transparency Trio. These three Information Technology experts, Gen. Brig. Eliseo Rio, Gus Lagman, and Franklin Ysaac, together with Col. Leonardo Odono, fearlessly led the fight for truth and justice by exposing the election fraud that led to Marcos-Duterte's victory.

With their formidable credentials, these men of honor and integrity, already in their late seventies, were willing to take up the cudgels for the nation. It has been a steep battle for them, but they have built a tight case, with evidence of direct fraud, including pre-loading and pre-programming of votes, possibly as high as 20 million votes, which will be proven beyond doubt by the transmission logs that the TNTrio are demanding. Comelec, however, has been dodging the pressure to publish these logs. After months of delays, it published instead reception logs, which, unwittingly prove the TNTrio's observations that the election was indeed rigged.

The TNTrio's latest analysis of the reception logs confirms and substantiates the International Observer Mission's conclusion that the National Elections of 2022 failed the Filipino people. Australian Senator Lee Rhiannon, a Commissioner of the UN International Observer Mission, declared: "The evidence is overwhelming… Marcos Jr. and Sara Duterte were not elected legitimately." On the strength of the IOM's findings, we are being governed by an illegitimate President and Vice President.

Filipinos in the Philippines and the Filipino Diaspora have joined forces and resources to support the movement for truth and transparency led by the

TNTrio. The Mandamus Group and Malaya New Jersey have sponsored two fora to raise awareness of the National Elections 2022 issues and are planning the third. They have also led a fundraising campaign and set up a Legal Fund for the TNTrio's Mandamus Petition now before the Supreme Court.

Furthermore, they have been trying to get as many signatures for the People's Mandamus Online Petition to put moral pressure on the Supreme Court to compel Comelec to produce true transmission logs. However, after more than a month, they have only been able to gather 20,000 signatures, which is short of the goal of at least 100,000 signatures needed for the petition to have considerable moral weight. We turn to you, VP Leni, to support the people's quest for the truth.

Given your influence on members of the Pink Movement, you would be able to gather millions of signatures. We ask you to organize and mobilize the leaders of your entire network, to gather signatures in support of the People's Mandamus Petition, and to join protest rallies, in support of the movement for truth and transparency.

We believe that signing the People's Mandamus Petition is an act of citizenship that every Filipino should take part in. Its aim is to compel Comelec to fulfill its constitutional duty to assure the Filipino people of the integrity of the May 9 elections by preserving and releasing genuine transmission logs in its possession needed to establish the veracity of the election results it had reported. The People's Mandamus Petition is our last line of defense for our democracy, the soul of which has been violated by credible evidence of electronic manipulation of vote results that the TNTrio have copiously demonstrated.

You have always espoused a leadership that is consultative, so that the voices of people from the ground can truly be heard and become the basis of your decisions. In this light, may we request that you have an audience with a representative group composed of

Filipinos from the Philippines and Filipino Diaspora through a zoom meeting, to discuss how we can all help build a new Philippines.

But in all of this, where are our Filipino youth in the fight for truth and justice? They seemed to have disengaged themselves from the affairs and concerns of the nation after the elections. But you inspired them. There was something about you and your rallying cry, "gobyernong tapat, lahat ay aangat," that moved their hearts and sparked their hope, even though they are cynical about politics and institutions. That same "something" that created the groundswell Pink Movement of volunteer citizens is a phenomenon that has never been seen before in Philippine politics.

We hold on to your words: "We have a lot to fight for...so we do not give up. Stay active, continue to fight for the truth" (May 10, 2022). Whenever we feel like giving up, we remember the old man who hobbled with one foot, supported by a crutch, to join the mammoth pink rally at Ortigas Avenue. He stood there under the heat to support you and the entire opposition, believing that the hope of the nation was there – "ang pagasa ay kulay rosas."

We must all channel that same spirit of hope and determination in our fight to defend our democracy. We believe that someday, we will have an answer to the questions of the boy and his sister – "What will happen to us now, Mom?" But for now, we have a battle to win, and win we must! But we can only win the battle with the overwhelming support of the Filipino people, which we hope you will help elicit.

Thank you, in anticipation of your help and support for the people's fight for truth and transparency and their right to information on matters of public concern as guaranteed by the Constitution.

In the end, the truth, and only the truth shall set us free.

Sincerely yours,
Ma. Christina Astorga, Ph.D

Oswald Magno, LL.B
Mila Magno
Ruben Guieb
Mandamus Group International
1521 SOLIDARITY FOR TRUTH AND JUSTICE (Manila, Philippines)
FAHRA (Filipino-American Human Rights Alliance)
GPDC (Global Pinoy Diaspora Canada)
LINGAP [Life Improvement Network for Grassroots Assistance and Progress] (Bulacan, Philippines)
Malaya, Canada
Malaya, New Jersey (USA)
Netizens for Courage and Bravery (NETCAB)
Pamana Cultural Association (Canada)
Brig.Gen. Eliseo M. Rio Jr. (Retired)
Franklin Ysaac
Gus Lagman
Leonardo Odoño (Colonel, ret.)
Mel Magdamo, LL.B
Fr. Albert E. Alejo, SJ
Fr. Robert Reyes
Fr. Victor de Jesus, STL, Th.D. Cand.

....

4

APPEAL TO THE ARMED FORCES OF THE PHILIPPINES AND THE PHILIPPINE NATIONAL POLICE ...

https://bit.ly/42padKs

https://bit.ly/OrgSupportMandamus
https://chng.it/79gg9SqWmq
Quo vadis, Filipinas ?

The military's constitutional duty is to serve, protect, and defend the Filipino people, guided by their core values of duty, honor, and integrity. Recent events emphasize the importance of reminding the military of their responsibility to the people.

It is crucial that the military fulfills their duty of protecting the Filipino's sovereign will in choosing the leaders of the nation. The sanctity of the ballot should be upheld at all times, and no institution, including the COMELEC, should undermine the people's sovereign will. Therefore, we urge the military to ensure that the people's voices are heard and their votes are counted fairly and accurately.

Furthermore, we must remind the military of their duty to observe their core value of honor. They must be solely guided by their constitutional duty, against the lure of money, power, or fame, to which many have fallen. As they stand and salute the flag, they are called to be true patriots, their highest vocation and mission.

Finally, we urge the military to uphold their core value of integrity by being the people's soldiers through their word and action. They must stand up for the people's basic human rights, particularly their fundamental right to truth and transparency of elections, which lies at the heart of democracy. By upholding these values, the military can best serve the Filipino people and protect their rights, ensuring a just and democratic society for all.

Signed by :
Ma. Christina Astorga, Ph.D
Oswald Magno, LL.B
Mila Magno
Ruben Guieb
Mandamus Group International
1521 SOLIDARITY FOR TRUTH AND JUSTICE
(Manila, Philippines)

FAHRA (Filipino-American Human Rights Alliance)

GPDC (Global Pinoy Diaspora Canada)

LINGAP [Life Improvement Network for Grassroots Assistance and Progress] (Bulacan, Philippines)

Malaya, Canada

Malaya, New Jersey (USA)

Netizens for Courage and Bravery (NETCAB)

Pamana Cultural Association (Canada)

Brig.Gen. Eliseo M. Rio Jr. (Retired)

Franklin Ysaac

Gus Lagman

Leonardo Odoño (Colonel, ret.)

Mel Magdamo, LL.B

Fr. Albert E. Alejo, SJ

Fr. Robert Reyes

Fr. Victor de Jesus, STL, Th.D. Cand.

... and many others ...

Please sign here to add your name and see the growing list of signatories:

https://bit.ly/42padKs

https://bit.ly/OrgSupportMandamus

https://bit.ly/mandamuspetition

MAGPIRMA rin po tayo sa PEOPLE'S MANDAMUS PETITION sa Change.Org. to compel Comelec to disclose the True Transmission Logs of the 2022 election.

MAG SIGN LANG PO. HUWAG NA MAG DONATE DITO SA CHANGE.ORG.

https://chng.it/79gg9SqWmq

You do not have to "CHIP IN" money. Instead share it to your family, friends and associates through FB, email, etc..

AFP MISSION
"Protect the people, secure the sovereignty of the State and the integrity of the national territory."

LOYALTY

HONOR
SERVICE
PATRIOTISM
ARMED FORCES OF THE PHILIPPINES
PROTECTING THE PEOPLE, SECURING THE STATE

....

5
Another suspicious data derived from the Reception Logs uploaded by COMELEC in its website on March 23, 2023. – TNTRIO Movement Group

In the May 9, 2022 Election, there were precincts where actual voters are MORE than the registered voters and a number of precincts overseas with exactly 999 people who actually voted out of 1000 registered voters.

There are now so many discrepancies (more are still to come) in that Reception Logs that COMELEC is actually showing the public its ineptness to come up with an accurate, clean and honest election.

That is why we DEMAND our right for Freedom Of Information that COMELEC shows the actual Transmission Logs corroborated by the Telcos' Call Detail Record (CDR), instead of deceiving the public with questionable Reception Logs they say are Transmission Logs.

MAY 9, 2022 NLE - ACTUAL VOTES VS. REGISTERED VOTERS - 99.9%

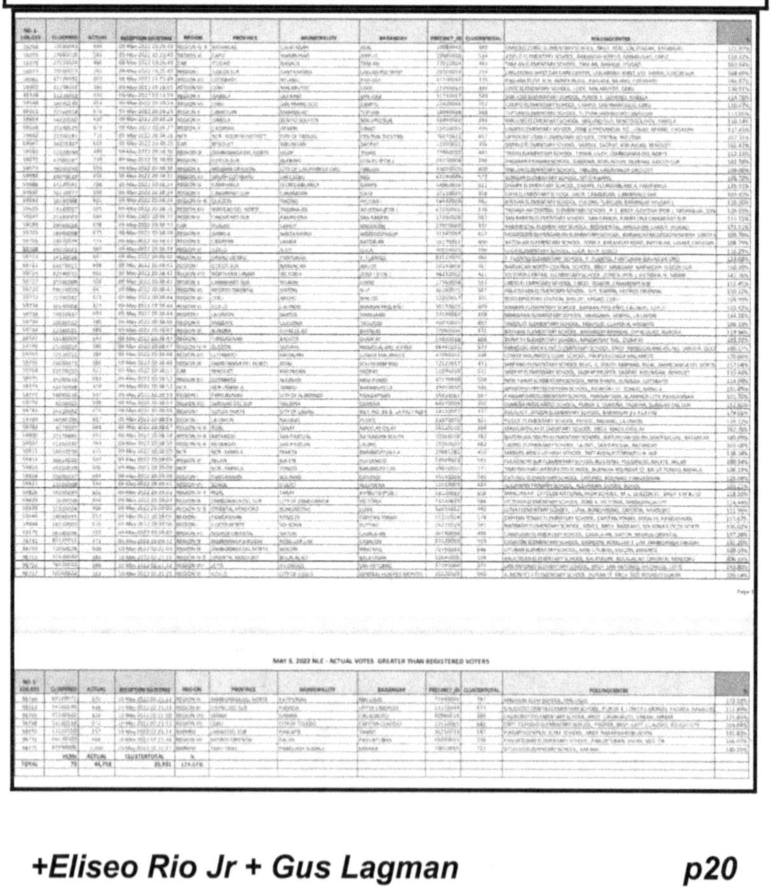

NO. 1-SOURCE	CLUSTERED	ACTUAL	RECEPTION DATE/TIME	REGION	PROVINCE	MUNICIPALITY	BARANGAY	PRECINCT_ID	CLUSTEREDVAL	POLLINGCENTER	%
[illegible]	[illegible]	[illegible]	[illegible]	[illegible]	[illegible]	[illegible]	[illegible]	[illegible]	[illegible]	[illegible]	[illegible]
	VOTES	ACTUAL		CLUSTEREDTOTAL		%					
TOTAL	[illegible]	[illegible]		[illegible]		[illegible]					

NO. 1-SOURCE	CLUSTERED	ACTUAL	RECEPTION DATE/TIME	REGION	PROVINCE	MUNICIPALITY	BARANGAY	PRECINCT_ID	CLUSTEREDVAL	POLLINGCENTER	%
[illegible]	[illegible]	[illegible]	[illegible]	[illegible]	[illegible]	[illegible]	[illegible]	[illegible]	[illegible]	[illegible]	[illegible]

MAY 9, 2022 NLE - ACTUAL VOTES GREATER THAN REGISTERED VOTERS

NO. 1-SOURCE	CLUSTERED	ACTUAL	RECEPTION DATE/TIME	REGION	PROVINCE	MUNICIPALITY	BARANGAY	PRECINCT_ID	CLUSTEREDTOTAL	POLLINGCENTER	%
[illegible]	[illegible]	[illegible]	[illegible]	[illegible]	[illegible]	[illegible]	[illegible]	[illegible]	[illegible]	[illegible]	[illegible]
	VOTES	ACTUAL		CLUSTERTOTAL		%					
TOTAL	[illegible]	[illegible]		[illegible]		[illegible]					

6
Here's the full text of the Manifestation and Motion of our Lawyer before the SC. – Franklin Ysaac – May 22, 2023

REPUBLIC OF THE PHILIPPINES
SUPREME COURT   2023 MAY 22 AM 11: 35
MANILA

En Banc

ELISEO MIJARES RIO JR.
AUGUSTO CADELIÑA LAGMAN
FRANKLIN FAYLOGA YSAAC,
            Petitioners,

-*versus*-   <u>**G.R. No. 263838**</u>

For: *Petition for Mandamus*
      with Prayer for Temporary
      Restraining Order

COMMISSION ON ELECTIONS
(COMELEC)
SMARTMATIC TOTAL
INFORMATION MANAGEMENT
DITO TELECOMMUNITY
GLOBE TELECOM
SMART COMMUNICATIONS,
            Respondents.
X--X

MANIFESTATION AND MOTION

        P e t i t i o n e r s , thru the undersigned counsel, respectfully manifest to the Honorable Court, in light of the Comment filed by the COMELEC dated April 3, 2023 (copy of which was not furnished to the undersigned counsel), as follows:

        1.   In the Comment of the COMELEC, it moves for dismissal of the Instant Petition on the ground of mootness, on the ground that:

        "4.   On 22 March 2023, the COMELEC released and uploaded in its official website the List of VCM Transmission Logs of the 9 May 2022 national and local elections. The COMELEC uploaded not only the files containing the "List of VCM Received During First Hour of Transmission May 9, 2022 NLE" which petitioners seek to be preserved, but also the "List of VCM Received Entire Transmission Logs May 9, 2022 NLE." The decision to make the data publicly available was to erase doubts on the credibility of the automated election system. With the publication of the transmission logs, the public can access more information regarding the election process, essential to guaranteeing accountability and transparency in the country's electoral system"

(Par. 4, Comment)

2.   While it is true that the COMELEC released and uploaded on its official website the list of transmission logs of the last national elections on May 9, 2022, it turned out that what was released were not transmission logs but reception logs as pleaded by the Petitioners in their Supplemental Petition;

3.   In any case, the reception logs shown to the public are full of discrepancies. There were several Election Results that were received in the Transparency Server even before these were transmitted by the precinct Vote Counting Machines. There were statistically IMPOSSIBLE data where the ratio of actual voters to registered voters are the same in several provinces and does not change in two successive hours. There are 113 precincts that have exactly 1,000 registered voters with all 1,000 voting or all 113 precincts have 100% voters' turnout;

4.   The data shown by the received Election Returns Transparency Server from 7:00PM of May 9, 2022 to the afternoon of May 13, 2022 DO NOT match the data shown in the Reception Logs uploaded in the website of COMELEC on March 23, 2023;

5.   In a forum conducted by COMELEC on October 18, 2022, a slide was shown entitled "Accumulated Vote Counting Machine Transmissions" that PEAKED at the SECOND HOUR after transmissions started which is in stark contrast with the FIRST HOUR after voting was closed;

6.   The starting time 7:08PM when the Transparency Server began receiving Vote Counting Machine transmissions indicated in the Reception Logs uploaded by COMELEC in their website on March 23, 2023, is IMPOSSIBLE. The nine major tasks required by COMELEC to be accomplished first before any Vote Counting Machine transmissions can start took at least 19 minutes to complete. The earliest Vote Counting Machine transmissions to be received would not be before 7:19PM. Closing the voting in precincts before the official time of 7:00PM is illegal because it might deprive a voter his/her right of suffrage;

7.   There was an unbelievable PEAK count of 20M+ votes shown to the public by the COMELEC Transparency Server at 8:02PM of May 9, 2022, just an hour after the voting was closed. And in that first hour, 9 major parties tasks have to be done first in all precincts that took at least 19 minutes BEFORE any Vote Counting Machine transmissions can start. Yet in the second hour, the Vote Counting Machine transmissions received unexplainably dropped to just 13.2M+;

8.   It may not be amiss to require that COMELEC must explain the gargantuan 28% increase of registered voters for the 2022 election, which is the highest in our electoral history. Increase in Voter Registration and increase in Total Population have been quite proportional for the past half century. The proportional increase had been averaging around just 3% range in between elections. In 2019, COMELEC delisted 10,483,214 voters bringing down registered voters to 51,364,557. Yet COMELEC registered a record of 14,384,972 during the pandemic years to come up with an unbelievable 65,745529 registered voters for the 2022 Election.

P R A Y E R

WHEREFORE, it is respectfully prayed that —

a)   The motion to dismiss filed by Respondent COMELEC be denied; and

b)   That the Honorable Court give due course to the Instant Petition;

Petitioners further pray for such further legal and equitable reliefs as may be necessary and proper in the premises.

Makati City for the City of Manila, May 19, 2023.

AGABIN VERZOLA & LAYAOEN
LAW OFFICE
Counsel for the Petitioners
26th Floor, Pacific Star Building
Gil Puyat Ave. cor. Makati Ave.
1200 Makati City
Tel. No. 8817-7717 ● Fax No. 7751-7951
Email: *averheldlaw@yahoo.com.ph*

By:

PACIFICO A. AGABIN
Roll of Attorneys No. 16609
IBP Lifetime No. 251
PTR No. MKT9569752/Jan. 10, 2023/Makati City
MCLE Exempt

Copy furnished via courier:

COMMISSION ON ELECTIONS
8/F Palacio del Gobernador
Andres Soriano corner General Luna
Intramuros 1002 Manila

SMARTMATIC TOTAL INFORMATION MANAGEMENT
Unit 2208 22/F The Trade and Financial Tower
7th Avenue corner 32nd Street
Bonifacio Global City
1634 Taguig

ERNESTO R. ALBERTO
DITO CME Holdings President
DITO TELE COMMUNITY
21st Floor UDENNA Tower
Rizal Drive corner 4th Avenue
Bonifacio Global City 1634 Taguig

ERNEST L. CU
Globe Telecom President
GLOBE TELECOM
Globe Tower @ 2nd Street corner 7th Avenue
Bonifacio Global City 1634 Taguig

Joint Congressional Oversight Committee on Automated Election System
(JCOC AES)
House of Representatives
Batasan Hills, Quezon City

OFFICE OF THE SOLICITOR GENERAL (OSG)
134 Amorsolo St., Legaspi Village
1229 Makati City

REPUBLIC OF THE PHILIPPINES
SUPREME COURT
MANILA

En Banc

**ELISEO MIJARES RIO JR.
AUGUSTO CADELIÑA LAGMAN
FRANKLIN FAYLOGA YSAAC,**
Petitioners,

-*versus*-

**COMMISSION ON ELECTIONS
(COMELEC)
SMARTMATIC TOTAL
INFORMATION MANAGEMENT
DITO TELECOMMUNITY
GLOBE TELECOM
SMART COMMUNICATIONS,**
Respondents.

G.R. No. 263838

For: *Petition for Mandamus with Prayer for Temporary Restraining Order*

x--x

MANIFESTATION AND MOTION

Petitioners, thru the undersigned counsel, respectfully manifest to the Honorable Court, in light of the Comment filed by the COMELEC dated April 3, 2023 (copy of which was not furnished to the undersigned counsel), as follows:

1.   In the Comment of the COMELEC, it moves for dismissal of the Instant Petition on the ground of mootness, on the ground that:

> "4.   On 22 March 2023, the COMELEC released and uploaded in its official website the List of VCM Transmission Logs of the 9 May 2022 national and local elections. The COMELEC uploaded not only the files containing the "List of VCM Received During First Hour of Transmission May 9, 2022 NLE"   which petitioners seek to be preserved, but also the "List of VCM Received Entire Transmission Logs May 9, 2022 NLE." The decision to make the data publicly available

was to erase doubts on the credibility of the automated
election system.   With the publication of the
transmission logs, the public can access more
information regarding the election process, essential to
guaranteeing accountability and transparency in the
country's electoral system"

(Par. 4, Comment)

2.   While it is true that the COMELEC released and uploaded on
its official website the list of transmission logs of the last national elections
on May 9, 2022, it turned out that what was released were not transmission
logs but reception logs as pleaded by the Petitioners in their Supplemental
Petition;

3.   In any case, the reception logs shown to the public are full of
discrepancies. There were several Election Results that were received in the
Transparency Server even before these were transmitted by the precinct Vote
Counting Machines. There were statistically IMPOSSIBLE data where the
ratio of actual voters to registered voters are the same in several provinces
and does not change in two successive hours. There are 113 precincts that
have exactly 1,000 registered voters with all 1,000 voting or all 113
precincts have 100% voters' turnout;

4.   The data shown by the received Election Returns Transparency
Server from 7:00PM of May 9, 2022 to the afternoon of May 13, 2022 DO
NOT match the data shown in the Reception Logs uploaded in the website of
COMELEC on March 23, 2023;

5.   In a forum conducted by COMELEC on October 18, 2022, a
slide was shown entitled "Accumulated Vote Counting Machine
Transmissions" that PEAKED at the SECOND HOUR after transmissions
started which is in stark contrast with the FIRST HOUR after voting was
closed;

6.   The starting time 7:08PM when the Transparency Server began
receiving Vote Counting Machine transmissions indicated in the Reception
Logs uploaded by COMELEC in their website on March 23, 2023, is
IMPOSSIBLE.   The nine major tasks required by COMELEC to be
accomplished first before any Vote Counting Machine transmissions can
start took at least 19 minutes to complete. The earliest Vote Counting
Machine transmissions to be received would not be before 7:19PM. Closing
the voting in precincts before the official time of 7:00PM is illegal because it
might deprive a voter his/her right of suffrage;

7.   There was an unbelievable PEAK count of 20M+ votes shown to the public by the COMELEC Transparency Server at 8:02PM of May 9, 2022, just an hour after the voting was closed. And in that first hour, 9 major parties tasks have to be done first in all precincts that took at least 19 minutes BEFORE any Vote Counting Machine transmissions can start. Yet in the second hour, the Vote Counting Machine transmissions received unexplainably dropped to just 13.2M+;

8.   It may not be amiss to require that COMELEC must explain the gargantuan 28% increase of registered voters for the 2022 election, which is the highest in our electoral history. Increase in Voter Registration and increase in Total Population have been quite proportional for the past half century. The proportional increase had been averaging around just 3% range in between elections. In 2019, COMELEC delisted 10,483,214 voters bringing down registered voters to 51,364,557. Yet COMELEC registered a record of 14,384,972 during the pandemic years to come up with an unbelievable 65,745529 registered voters for the 2022 Election.

PRAYER

WHEREFORE, it is respectfully prayed that —

a)   The motion to dismiss filed by Respondent COMELEC be denied; and

b)   That the Honorable Court give due course to the Instant Petition;

Petitioners further pray for such further legal and equitable reliefs as may be necessary and proper in the premises.

Makati City for the City of Manila, May 19, 2023.

AGABIN VERZOLA & LAYAOEN
LAW OFFICE
Counsel for the Petitioners
26th Floor, Pacific Star Building
Gil Puyat Ave. cor. Makati Ave.
1200 Makati City
Tel. No. 8817-7717 • Fax No. 7751-7951
Email: *averhelallaw@yahoo.com.ph*

Manifestation and Motion
Eliseo Mijares Rio Jr., Augusto Cadeliña Lagman,
Franklin Faylaga Ysaac vs. COMELEC, et al.
G.R. No. 263838
Page | 4

By:

PACIFICO A. AGABIN
Roll of Attorneys No. 16609
IBP Lifetime No. 251
PTR No. MKT9569752/Jan. 10, 2023/Makati City
MCLE Exempt

Copy furnished via courier:

COMMISSION ON ELECTIONS
8/F Palacio del Gobernador
Andres Soriano corner General Luna
Intramuros 1002 Manila

SMARTMATIC TOTAL INFORMATION MANAGEMENT
Unit 2208 22/F The Trade and Financial Tower
7th Avenue corner 32nd Street
Bonifacio Global City
1634 Taguig

ERNESTO R. ALBERTO
DITO CME Holdings President
DITO TELE COMMUNITY
21st Floor UDENNA Tower
Rizal Drive corner 4th Avenue
Bonifacio Global City 1634 Taguig

ERNEST L. CU
Globe Telecom President
GLOBE TELECOM
Globe Tower @ 2nd Street corner 7th Avenue
Bonifacio Global City 1634 Taguig

Joint Congressional Oversight Committee on Automated Election System
(JCOC AES)
House of Representatives
Batasan Hills, Quezon City

OFFICE OF THE SOLICITOR GENERAL (OSG)
134 Amorsolo St., Legaspi Village
1229 Makati City

....

7
PREPONDERANCE OF EVIDENCE SHOWS THAT THE MAY 09, 2022 ELECTION WAS RIGGED. – Eliseo Rio Jr. – May 22, 2023

1. COMELEC must explain the gargantuan 28% increase of registered voters for the 2022 election, which is the highest in our electoral history. Increase in Voter Registration and increase in Total Population have been quite proportional for the past half century. The proportional increase had been averaging around just 3% range in between elections. In 2019, COMELEC delisted 10,483, 214 voters bringing down registered voters to 51,364,557. Yet COMELEC registered a record of 14,384,972 during the pandemic years to come up with an unbelievable 65,745,529 registered voters for the 2022 Election.

2. On March 09, 2022, the Parish Pastoral Council on Responsible Voting (PPCRV) and NAMFREL claimed a lack of transparency in the printing of ballots and configuration of Secure Digital (SD) Cards, because they have not been allowed to observe inside the National Printing Office and the COMELEC warehouse in Sta.Rosa, Laguna, as ordered by Comm. Marlon Casquejo, in compliance with the COVID restrictions. 66.4% of the ballots have been printed, with 32% being sent for packing and shipping. The Senate also criticized the COMELEC's decision to downscale the implementation of digital signatures to selected areas only, when it was earlier announced that ALL Electoral Boards will digitally sign the Electoral Returns.

3. On March 22, 2022, NAMFREL discovered that the VCM Source Code differed in its the Hash Code. The human-readable source code consists of commands to the VCMs written by programmers. The hash code is a computer-generated "fingerprint" of the software. If a change in the software is introduced, a different hash code will be generated. NAMFREL emailed Comm. Marlon Casquejo but did not reply, and instead posted on the COMELEC website an admission of its international certifier Pro V&V of human typographical error. NAMFREL averred that their excuse was flimsy because IT professionals should just "copy-paste" electronic documents. They again wrote Comm. Casquejo on March 25 seeking five (5) documents that pertained to Pro V&V's encoding and compliance with hash code protocols for independent verification, but COMELEC did not reply. Up to this date, no satisfactory explanation had begun given by COMELEC regarding this matter.

4. The Commission on Elections and its automated election system provider, Smartmatic, have made a change in their protocols, which prevented the tracing of the actual source of transmission of votes from precincts that can potentially be used to tamper with the results as warned by then Senate President Tito Sotto and Senator Ping Lacson.

5. There was an unbelievable PEAK count of 20M+ votes shown to the public by the COMELEC Transparency Server at 8:02PM of May 9, 2022, just an hour after the voting closed. In that first hour, nine (9) major tasks have to be done first in all precincts that took at least 19 minutes BEFORE any VCM transmissions can start. Yet in the second hour, when logically all precincts' Electoral Boards should have accomplished the 9 tasks, the VCM transmissions received unexplainably dropped to just 13.2M+. Also, there occurred a statistically highly improbable constant vote ratio among ALL TEN candidates for Presidency and

NINE candidates for VP, NOT ONLY between two candidates.

6. COMELEC cannot assure the voting public by actual sworn statements from watchdogs NAMFREL/LENTE and/or political parties that the integrity of the ballots brought from the different precincts to Diamond Hotel for the Random Manual Audit (RMA) was intact and had never been tampered while in transit.

7. In a forum conducted by COMELEC on October 18, 2022, a slide entitled "Accumulated VCM Transmissions" showed that transmissions PEAKED at the SECOND HOUR, which is in stark contrast with the FIRST HOUR PEAK shown by the Transparency Server after voting closed.

8. The starting time of 7:08:50PM, when the Transparency Server began receiving VCM transmissions as indicated in the Reception Logs uploaded by COMELEC in their website on March 23, 2023, is IMPOSSIBLE. The 9 major tasks required by COMELEC to be accomplished first before any VCM transmissions can start, took at least 19 minutes to complete, with the printing of 8 copies of the Election Returns alone taking 12 minutes. The earliest VCM transmissions to be received could not be before 7:19PM. Closing the voting in precincts before the official time of 7:00PM is illegal because it might deprive a voter of his/her right of suffrage.

9. The Mandamus Petition docketed in the Supreme Court (SC) on Nov. 03, 2022 is for the preservation of Transmission Logs and the Call Detail Records kept by the three (3) Telecommunications Companies. The SC ordered the respondent COMELEC to comment on our petition last January 22, 2023, but instead of answering directly the SC, COMELEC told the SC that since it had already uploaded the Transmission Logs in its website, the petition becomes moot and academic. COMELEC is deceiving the SC because what it uploaded is the Reception Logs, NOT the Transmission Logs which is the subject of the petition.

10. The Reception Logs shown to the public are full of discrepancies.

a) There were several Election Results that were received by the Transparency Server even BEFORE these were transmitted by the precinct VCMs.

b) There were statistically IMPOSSIBLE data where the ratio of actual voters to registered voters are the same in several provinces and does not change in two successive hours.

c) There are 113 precincts that have exactly 1,000 registered voters with all 1,000 voting or all 113 precincts have 100% voter's turnout.

d) There are a number of overseas precincts with exactly 999 actual voters out of 1,000 registered voters.

e) There were also numerous local precincts whose actual voters are MORE THAN the number of registered voters.

11. The data shown by the received ERs of the Transparency Server from 7:00PM of May 9th to the afternoon of May 13th, DO NOT MATCH the data shown in the Reception Logs uploaded in the website of COMELEC on March 23, 2023.

The 2022 Election was so manipulated that by 9pm of May 9, 2022, "TAPOS NA ANG BOKSING" as to who won for President and VP.

PS. Shown here are video clips that will prove that it takes at least 12 minutes to print the 8 copies both the National and Local Election Returns (ERs) and sample pictures that illustrate the preponderance of evidence.

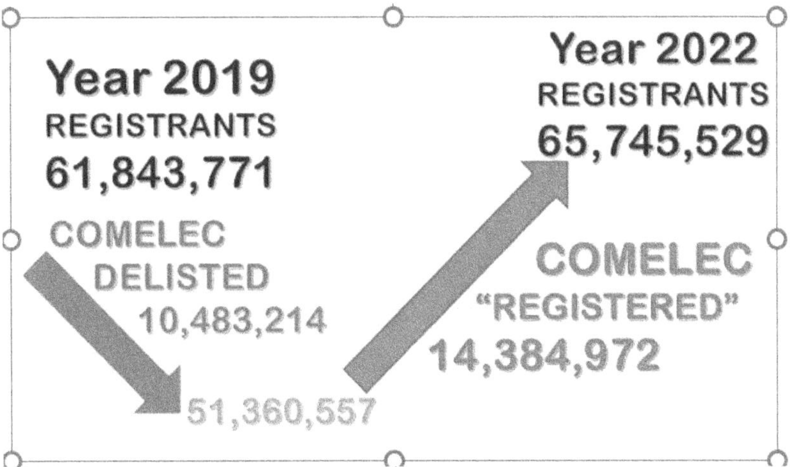

Year 2019 REGISTRANTS 61,843,771

COMELEC DELISTED 10,483,214

51,360,557

Year 2022 REGISTRANTS 65,745,529

COMELEC "REGISTERED" 14,384,972

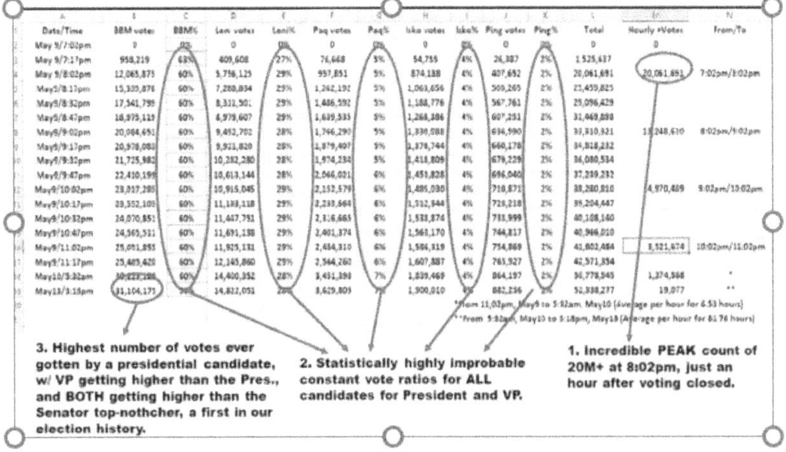

Date/Time	BBM votes	BBM%	Leni votes	Leni%	Paq votes	Paq%	Isko votes	Isko%	Ping votes	Ping%	Total	Hourly #Votes	From/To
May 9/7:02pm	0	0%	0	0%	0	0%	0	0%	0	0%	0	0	
May 9/7:17pm	958,219	63%	409,608	27%	76,668	5%	54,755	4%	26,387	2%	1,525,637		
May 9/8:02pm	12,065,875	60%	5,756,125	29%	957,851	5%	874,188	4%	407,652	2%	20,061,691	20,061,691	7:02pm/8:02pm
May9/8:17pm	15,335,876	60%	7,280,034	29%	1,262,192	5%	1,063,656	4%	509,265	2%	23,459,825		
May9/8:32pm	17,541,799	60%	8,331,501	29%	1,486,592	5%	1,188,776	4%	567,761	2%	25,096,429		
May9/8:47pm	18,975,113	60%	8,979,607	29%	1,639,535	5%	1,264,386	4%	607,251	2%	31,469,898		
May9/9:02pm	20,084,651	60%	9,452,702	28%	1,766,290	5%	1,330,088	4%	634,990	2%	33,310,921	13,248,610	8:02pm/9:02pm
May9/9:17pm	20,978,083	60%	9,921,820	28%	1,879,407	5%	1,374,744	4%	660,178	2%	34,818,232		
May9/9:32pm	21,725,982	60%	10,282,280	28%	1,974,234	5%	1,418,809	4%	679,229	2%	36,080,534		
May9/9:47pm	22,410,199	60%	10,613,144	28%	2,066,021	6%	1,451,828	4%	696,040	2%	37,239,232		
May9/10:02pm	23,017,285	60%	10,915,045	29%	2,152,579	6%	1,486,030	4%	718,871	2%	38,280,810	4,970,489	9:02pm/10:02pm
May9/10:17pm	23,552,108	60%	11,188,118	29%	2,233,664	6%	1,512,544	4%	728,218	2%	39,204,647		
May9/10:32pm	24,070,851	60%	11,447,751	29%	2,316,665	6%	1,533,874	4%	731,999	2%	40,108,140		
May9/10:47pm	24,365,511	60%	11,691,138	29%	2,401,374	6%	1,561,170	4%	744,817	2%	40,966,010		
May9/11:02pm	25,051,855	60%	11,925,131	29%	2,484,310	6%	1,586,319	4%	754,869	2%	41,802,484	3,521,674	10:02pm/11:02pm
May9/11:17pm	25,485,425	60%	12,145,860	29%	2,544,262	6%	1,607,887	4%	761,927	2%	42,571,854		
May10/5:32am	30,423,186	60%	14,400,352	28%	3,431,391	7%	1,839,469	4%	864,197	2%	56,778,545	1,374,568	*
May13/3:18pm	31,104,175	79%	14,822,051	28%	3,629,803	7%	1,900,010	4%	882,256	2%	52,338,277	19,077	**

*From 11:02pm, May9 to 5:02am, May10 (Average per hour for 6.53 hours)
**From 5:02am, May10 to 3:18pm, May13 (Average per hour for 81.76 hours)

3. Highest number of votes ever gotten by a presidential candidate, w/ VP getting higher than the Pres., and BOTH getting higher than the Senator top-notcher, a first in our election history.

2. Statistically highly improbable constant vote ratios for ALL candidates for President and VP.

1. Incredible PEAK count of 20M+ at 8:02pm, just an hour after voting closed.

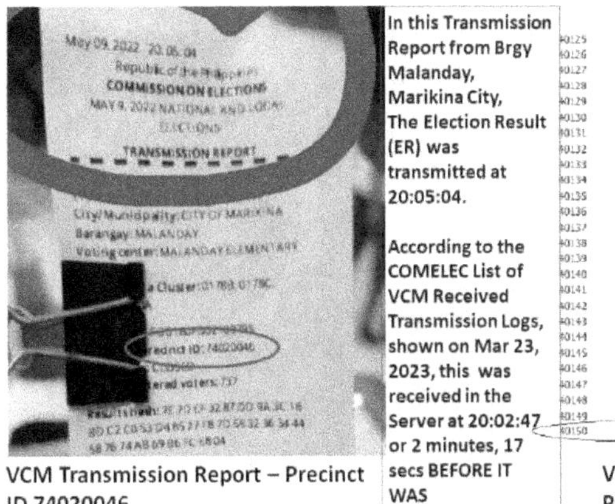

In this Transmission Report from Brgy Malanday, Marikina City, The Election Result (ER) was transmitted at 20:05:04.

According to the COMELEC List of VCM Received Transmission Logs, shown on Mar 23, 2023, this was received in the Server at 20:02:47 or 2 minutes, 17 secs BEFORE IT WAS TRANSMITTED.

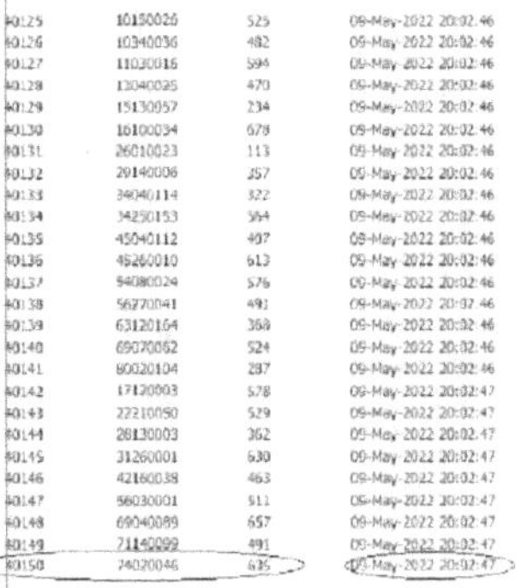

40125	10150026	525	09-May-2022 20:02.46
40126	10340036	482	09-May-2022 20:02.46
40127	11030016	594	09-May-2022 20:02.46
40128	13040025	470	09-May-2022 20:02.46
40129	15130057	234	09-May-2022 20:02.46
40130	16100034	678	09-May-2022 20:02.46
40131	26010023	113	09-May-2022 20:02.46
40132	29140006	357	09-May-2022 20:02.46
40133	34040114	322	09-May-2022 20:02.46
40134	34250153	564	09-May-2022 20:02.46
40135	45040112	407	09-May-2022 20:02.46
40136	45260010	613	09-May-2022 20:02.46
40137	54080024	576	09-May-2022 20:02.46
40138	56270041	491	09-May-2022 20:02.46
40139	63120164	368	09-May-2022 20:02.46
40140	69070062	524	09-May-2022 20:02.46
40141	80020104	287	09-May-2022 20:02.46
40142	17120003	578	09-May-2022 20:02.47
40143	22210050	529	09-May-2022 20:02.47
40144	28130003	362	09-May-2022 20:02.47
40145	31260001	630	09-May-2022 20:02.47
40146	42160038	463	09-May-2022 20:02.47
40147	56030001	511	09-May-2022 20:02.47
40148	69040089	657	09-May-2022 20:02.47
40149	71140099	491	09-May-2022 20:02.47
40150	74020046	635	09-May-2022 20:02.47

VCM Transmission Report – Precinct ID 74020046
Transmitted Time – 20:05:04

VCM Reception Report – Precinct ID 74020046
Received Time – 20:02:47

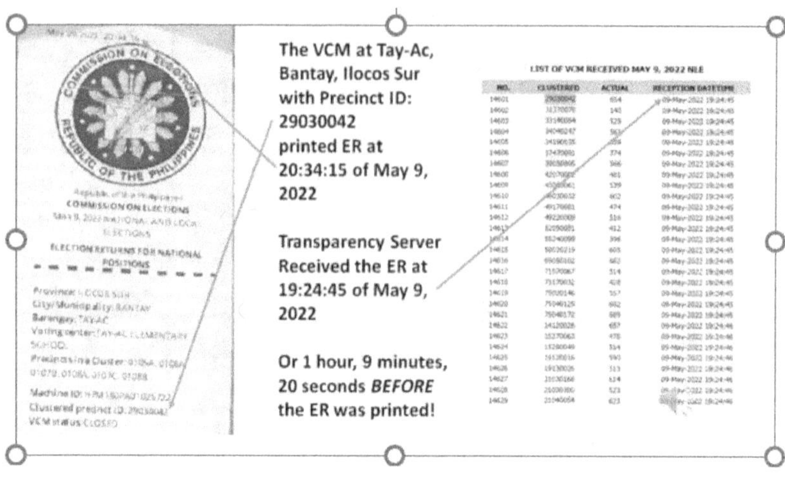

LIST OF VCM RECEIVED MAY 9, 2022 NLE

NO.	CLUSTERED	ACTUAL	RECEPTION DATETIME
14601	29030042	654	09-May-2022 19:24:45
14602	31370070	143	09-May-2022 19:24:45
14603	33140084	525	09-May-2022 19:24:45
14604	34040247	563	09-May-2022 19:24:45
14605	34190635	609	09-May-2022 19:24:45
14606	37470090	374	09-May-2022 19:24:45
14607	39030065	566	09-May-2022 19:24:45
14608	42070002	481	09-May-2022 19:24:45
14609	45080061	539	09-May-2022 19:24:45
14610	46030052	602	09-May-2022 19:24:45
14611	49170081	474	09-May-2022 19:24:45
14612	49220009	516	09-May-2022 19:24:45
14613	62090081	412	09-May-2022 19:24:45
14614	65240098	396	09-May-2022 19:24:45
14615	50020219	605	09-May-2022 19:24:45
14616	69080162	662	09-May-2022 19:24:45
14617	71570067	514	09-May-2022 19:24:45
14618	73170032	428	09-May-2022 19:24:45
14619	79020146	557	09-May-2022 19:24:45
14620	75040125	662	09-May-2022 19:24:45
14621	75040172	689	09-May-2022 19:24:46
14622	14120026	657	09-May-2022 19:24:46
14623	15270063	478	09-May-2022 19:24:46
14624	17200049	514	09-May-2022 19:24:46
14625	19130016	593	09-May-2022 19:24:46
14626	19130026	513	09-May-2022 19:24:46
14627	21030166	624	09-May-2022 19:24:46
14628	25030300	523	09-May-2022 19:24:46
14629	25040054	623	09-May-2022 19:24:46

....

8
MANDAMUS CASE. Comelec is like a fish caught by its mouth – Oswald Magno – May23, 2023

Their voluntarily publishing transmission logs, even though deficient, is an acknowledgment of the body's constitutional duty to protect the integrity of the ballot and to make available information when people have concerns about election results. The only issue now is the release of genuine transmission logs. They can no longer argue that the public is entitled only to reception logs, but not transmission logs. That would be an untenable, unsupportable argument.

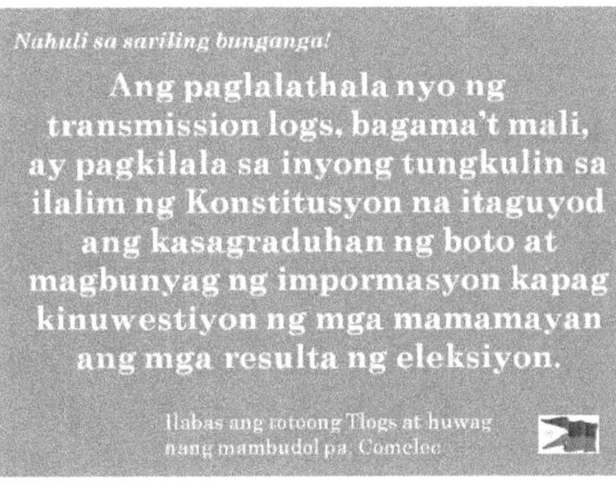

....

9
Homily by Franklin Ysaac – May 21, 2023

When you are sick, you need the best doctor to attend to your ailment . When you are failing in your studies, you need the best tutor to help you in your homework . When you are being bullied, you don't fight and you get the best martial artist. When a member of your family is being accused of falsehood in your school, you get your siblings who are also in the faculty to defend you . When you fail to get the course you want, try another course you like . When your friends dislike you, ignore them as they are not your true friends. When you keep company of bad people, you can become one of them. When your colleagues in your work are dishonest and are doing irregular matters, report them and if unsuccessful, find another job. When things are not working well at home, find the time to patch things up. If unsuccessful, let them be and leave home. When you feel there are anomalies being committed in your country, be resolute and find the time to be with people who will disclose and dispense with these anomalies.When your life is being threatened because of being whistleblower or accuser, be calm and find legal means to keep you safe and fight back.

When you have committed wrongdoings, open up and admit them and then do restitution to clear your conscience.

Always keep on praying your daily Rosary, attend daily mass, make the novena as this is your only way of opening conversation with the Good Lord.

Remember, He is always around and He will keep you company and safe from evil people if you always remember Him wherever and however your situation is.

Prayers are our windows and we have direct communication to Him faster than our computers or vcms or servers !

Today is Sunday and it is His Day!

Tomorrow is another day and we need to finish the tasks given to us !

Amen .

....

10
Maharlika Fund – Justified Plunder – Franklin Ysaac – May 25, 2023

There's no stopping this train of more plunder of government financial institutions which we already covered here .

Former DG Diwa Guinigundo and I delivered our positions against this Maharlika Fund a couple of months ago upon invitation by Finex Cebu.

Just our final words on this Maharlika fund:

1. Government is so bankrupt that it justifies passage of Maharlika fund as solution to finding funds for another round of granting behest grants and loans which will never be repaid.

2.Using funds from DBP, Landbank and even Bangko Central Bank is abuse and a graft case being committed by Congress and Senate as these are violations of the charters of these independent GFIs.

3. This government is running out of options of raising funds to replenish its depleted treasury from the international market . The foreign trips including the trip to Switzerland where he prematurely announced this Maharlika was a sovereign fund was the country's answer to its economic difficulties.

4: The Maharlika fund is his justification for his foreign trips and his failure to make foreign pledges a reality as foreign lenders doubt his legitimacy.

5. As graft case, the people can file another constituonal case before the SC to stop this Maharlika fund.

With gargantuan budget deficit, ballooning trade and balance of payments deficit, the non economists are tapping the GFI funds which are already being utilized for lending to developmental projects.

This robbing of funds from these GFIs is another form of creating another GFI which is illegal as it is taking what belongs to Juan and giving it to Pedro. Juan's funds are provided in charter approved by Congress. There are restrictions provided in the charter. Now, this Maharlika funds being railroaded do not have any railguards to protect the same funds.

Question : Who is the owner of Maharlika funds ? If the owners are the contributors namely DBP Landbank and Bangko Sentral bank, then the administrators of this fund should be the boards of these GFIs. In short, Maharlika find will just be subsidiary of the consortium or syndicate of GFIs . Rules governing funds contributed by GFIs should apply.

Read carefully the Maharlika bill and check if these questions are answered . If not, then this is a legalized plunder which should be brought to SC and be dismissed immediately.

Senate President Juan Miguel Zubiri (L) and House Speaker Martin Romualdez (R) congratulate President Ferdinand Marcos Jr (C) after he delivered his first State of the Nation address at the House of Representatives in Quezon City on Monday, July 25, 2022.

MANILA, Philippines **(Updated 4:31 p.m.)** — President Ferdinand "Bongbong" Marcos Jr. has certified the Senate bill seeking to create the Maharlika Investment Fund as urgent, which will allow the swifter passage of the measure in the chamber.

Marcos' certification of Senate Bill 2020, which is currently under the period of interpellations, was read out by Senate secretary Renato Bantug Jr. as part of the Wednesday session's reference of business.

....

11
Appeal to the All Opposition - Tina A. Astorga

APPEAL TO THE OPPOSITION, CURRENT ADMINISTRATION, THE CBCP, FAITH-BASED

COMMUNITIES, THE MILITARY, UNIVERSITIES AND COLLEGES, THE FILIPINO YOUTH, AND WHISTLEBLOWERS

APPEAL TO OPPOSITION

We supported you tirelessly, enduring both rain and sun for long hours. We placed our faith in you, risking everything for your cause.

You doubtless have heard of the TNTrio, three men who have in-depth knowledge of electoral processes and related computer systems. Their analyses of the May 9, 2022 election results palpably demonstrate that the recent elections were stolen from us, and despite the strong prima facie and direct evidence of electronic manipulation of vote results, COMELEC refuses to release the transmission logs that would prove it beyond any doubt.

The International Observer Mission has declared that the 2022 elections failed the Filipino people, with Marcos and Duterte having been elected illegitimately. The TNTrio's analyses have confirmed and substantiated direct fraud in the elections. What is also highly questionable is the number of registered voters for the 2022 election.

COMELEC must explain the gargantuan 28% increase of registered voters for the 2022 election, which is the highest in our electoral history. Increase in Voter Registration and increase in Total Population have been quite proportional for the past half century. The proportional increase had been averaging around just 3% range in between elections. In 2019, COMELEC delisted 10,483, 214 voters bringing down registered voters to 51,364,557. Yet COMELEC registered a record of 14,384,972 voters during the pandemic years to come up with an unbelievable 65,745,529 registered voters for the 2022 Election. What makes this doubly unbelievable is that this highest increase of registered voters in our electoral history happened during the pandemic years!

Despite these desecrations of our democracy, we have yet to hear a single word of protest from you. You have neither made any demands of Comelec to act with complete transparency nor supported the people's constitutionally guaranteed right to information on matters of public concern being pursued on the people's behalf in the Supreme Court by the TNTrio. Martin Luther King, Jr. once said, "A time comes when silence is betrayal."

Why have you left us to fight alone? Why have you abandoned us, the very people who once believed in your integrity and courage as leaders? We look to you to support us in this fight. We trust you will heed our call.

APPEAL TO THE CURRENT ADMINISTRATION

You came to power with the message of unity. Unity, however, can only be attained when we are bound by the same law that is founded on truth and based on justice. Regardless of differences of worldviews and ideologies, we are all required to obey the law.

It is the law that protects our basic human rights, one of which is the right to truth and transparency of elections, on which stands our democracy. The legality of your administration, however, has come under a cloud because of evidence purporting to show fraud.

Please recognize that you can govern more effectively if the people's concerns about the legitimacy of your administration are erased. It would not only be your victory, but it would be the triumph of democracy. It would be good for the country, to be under a government duly recognized by all its citizens.

We appeal to you to join us in the search for the truth, by supporting the Writ of Mandamus Petition now before the Supreme Court as well as the people's growing clamor to compel COMELEC to release the transmission logs, which can finally determine whether the elections were fair and honest and reflective of the true will of voters. We call on you to urge COMELEC to be transparent and to voluntarily release information that resolves the brewing controversy once and for all.

APPEAL TO THE CBCP: THE CALL TO CONSCIENCE

The church has a crucial role to play as the nation's conscience. In the 1986 Edsa revolution, the CBCP stood at the forefront, as the only institution capable of opposing the Marcos dictatorship and mobilizing the people to fight for their freedom. The CBCP proclaimed that the Marcos government had lost its moral right to rule due to fraud and deception.

We call upon the CBCP to once again awaken the nation's conscience. The UN International Observer Mission has declared that the 2022 elections failed the Filipino people, with Marcos and Duterte having been elected illegitimately. The TNTrio's analyses of early vote results as well as the improbable constant vote ratios among the candidates for national positions supports and substantiates this claim, which is corroborated by documentary evidence of electoral fraud.

We commend the CBCP for collaborating with the TNTRio and for educating and raising awareness among the people of God through the BECs regarding the 2022 elections and the urgent need to transform the nation's political culture.

It is the demand of the Gospel and Catholic social teaching for the CBCP to put its institutional moral weight behind the pursuit of truth and justice in relation to the 2022 elections, through an official statement urging the Comelec and the rest of officialdom to act in a forthright, prompt and transparent to accede to the people's demands to know the truth about the dubious May 9 election results.

As our shepherds, we look to the CBCP for moral guidance and leadership during this time of uncertainty, when our north star has dimmed, and all seems lost.

APPEAL TO FAITH-BASED COMMUNITIES

Religion wields a powerful force in politics, shaping social virtues of community, solidarity, and hope. Regardless of varying beliefs, ethical systems and spiritual practices, all faith-based communities share the pursuit of truth and justice.

We call on all Filipino men and women of different religions to live out their faith by fighting for truth and transparency in the 2022 elections. The love of God and our fellow citizens should manifest in our social and political engagements, as the pursuit of justice is an integral part of faith.

People of faith in churches, temples and mosques should work for the common good and social transformation. We exhort them to be agents of justice and bearers of hope in a nation that is fractured, divided and exploited. During the national crisis of 1986, Filipinos turned to their faith to win the revolution without a single bullet being fired. May this same faith guide our nation through the current crisis and lead us to a future filled with hope.

We urge all faith-based communities to unite as networks of solidarity in our collective endeavor for truth and justice.

APPEAL TO THE MILITARY

The military's constitutional duty is to serve, protect, and defend the Filipino people, guided by their core values of duty, honor, and integrity. Recent events emphasize the importance of reminding the military of their responsibility to the people.

It is crucial that the military fulfills their duty of protecting the Filipino's sovereign will in choosing the leaders of the nation. The sanctity of the ballot should be upheld at all times, and no institution, including the COMELEC, should undermine the people's sovereign will. Therefore, we urge the military to ensure that the people's voices are heard and their votes are counted fairly and accurately.

Furthermore, we must remind the military of their duty to observe their core value of honor. They must be solely guided by their constitutional duty, against the lure of money, power, or fame, to which many have fallen. As they stand and salute the flag, they are called to be true patriots, their highest vocation and mission.

Finally, we urge the military to uphold their core value of integrity by being the people's soldiers through their word and action. They must stand up for the people's basic human rights, particularly their fundamental right to truth and transparency of elections, which lies at the heart of democracy. By upholding these values, the military can best serve the Filipino people and protect their rights, ensuring a just and democratic society for all.

APPEAL TO COLLEGES AND UNIVERSITIES

Worldviews, thought systems, and ideologies compete for the minds and hearts of students. Colleges and universities are centers of learning, where students are educated to be critical and creative thinkers, who are able to navigate diverse perspectives in their pursuit of truth and justice.

We urge these institutions to fulfill their mission by providing students an integral, comprehensive, and holistic education that forms intellectually honest individuals with moral values and spiritual grounding. As the formators of the youth, colleges and universities are the bedrock of the nation's future.

We urge them to eradicate historical revisions and distortions in their curriculum which result in the mis-education of the Filipino youth, and to prevent the instrumentalization of colleges and universities as tools of ideology, of whatever persuasion, violating the true essence of a free and liberal education.

And finally, we exhort them to instill in our youth the ideals and values of our Filipino tradition, history, and culture, so that proud of their heritage, they may aspire to be true patriots, in the fight for truth, transparency and justice, and in the creation of a just Filipino society, that prioritizes the needs of the poor and marginalized.

APPEAL TO THE FILIPINO YOUTH

Filipino men and women, in their 70s and early 80s, are on the frontlines of the battle for democracy and social justice. Despite being battle-weary from their own struggles and those of the nation, they continue to fight with all their remaining strength and determination.

But where are the Filipino youth in the fight for truth, transparency and freedom of information now being waged by the TNTrio? They were once the driving force behind the First Quarter Storm and the inspiring energy of the Pink Revolution, the groundswell movement of volunteer citizens that was never seen before in Philippine politics. Singing and dancing to the inspiring message of "gobyernong tapat, angat buhay lahat," they embodied the nation's future and hope.

Regrettably, the moment seems fleeting as their passion and spirit have waned. The elections have seemingly disheartened them, leading them to retreat into their own world, disconnected from national concerns and affairs, leaving a void that only they can fill.

We urgently implore the Filipino youth to return to the fight. There are battles to be fought and victories to be won. We beseech them to join the CBCP and all democracy-loving Filipinos in supporting the work of TNTRio, condemning the rigging of elections 2022, holding the Comelec accountable, supporting the Mandamus Petition now pending in the Supreme Court, and signing the People's Mandamus (Online) Petition.

Be of brave heart, for this fight will be long and hard. You, whose forbears are Rizal, Bonifacio, and Mabini, are called to be patriots and heroes. Let your passion and spirit reignite the movement and fight for the soul of our democracy.

APPEAL TO WHISTLEBLOWERS

Fraud, especially fraud that is systematic and far reaching, cannot be done by a single person. Somewhere, someone who has been part of the scheme of this election deceit could be hiding and holding the truth from our people.

A crime committed against the Filipino people in the dark must be brought to light. A lie hidden in the secrecy of deceit must be exposed. Whistleblowers who know of this crime, and are a witness to this lie, cannot bear them on their conscience for long. If they bring these to their grave, even there they would not find peace.

We appeal, in the name of your God-given dignity and of your love for our people, and for your family, and for the sake of your peace, come out and take a stand. How long would you be able to hide the truth you know, when the burden of truth is too heavy for one to carry?

Be the conscience of our nation. Take the heroic act. Speak! Your word shall be the nation's life, your truth shall be the nation's hope. If only for this one noble act of courage, your life shall find its ultimate meaning.

PLEASE SHARE THIS POST. PLease sign the People's Mandamus to pressure SC to compel Comelec to release the transmission logs.

SIGNED BY:

List of Signatories

FILIPINO TRANSLATION:

APPEAL TO THE OPPOSITION, CURRENT ADMINISTRATION, THE CBCP, FAITH-BASED COMMUNITIES, THE MILITARY, UNIVERSITIES AND COLLEGES, THE FILIPINO YOUTH, AND WHISTLEBLOWERS

APPEAL TO THE OPPOSITION LEADERS

Kami ay sumuporta sa inyo ng walang kapaguran, tiniis ang tindi ng init ng araw at bugso ng ulan ng maraming oras. Ibinuhos naming ang pagtitiwala sa inyo, at sinuong namin ang lahat ng panganib para sa inyong layunin.

Siguradong narinig na ninyo ang TNTrio, ang tatlong kalalakihan na may malalim na kaalaman sa mga proceso ng halalan at ng mga sistema ng computer. Ang kanilang pagsusuri sa resulta ng halalan noong Mayo 09, 2022 ay malinaw na pinakita, na ang nagdaang halalan ay NINAKAW SA ATIN, ngunit kahit malakas ang mga prima facie at direct na ebidensiya ng electronic manipulation ng mga boto, ayaw pa rin ng

COMELEC ilabas ang Transmission Logs na magpapatunay nito, lampas sa anumang pagdududa.

Ang International Observer Mission ay idineklara na ang Halalan 2022 ay binigo ang Sambayanang Pilipino, at sina Marcos at Duterte ay nailuklok sa hindi lehitimong paraan. Ang pagsusuri ng TNTrio ang nag-kumpirma at nag-patunay na may tuwirang dayaan sa halalang ito. Ang isa pang kaduda-dudang pangyayari ay ang dami ng rehistradong botante para sa Halalan 2022.

Kailangan ipaliwanag ng COMELEC ang napakalaking karagdagan na 28% sa mga rehistradong botante, at ito ang pinaka-mataas sa kasaysayan ng halalan sa Pilipinas. Ang dagdag sa mga Rehistradong Botante ay proporsiyonado sa dagdag sa populasyon ng bansa sa nakaraang limampung (50) taon. Ang average ng proporsyonadong dagdag ay nasa 3% lamang sa pagitan ng bawat halalan. Noong 2019, tinanggal ng COMELEC ay 10,483,214 na botante, kaya bumaba sa 51,364,557 ang mga rehistrado. Ngunit nakapag-rehistro ang COMELEC ng di-karaniwang 14,384,972 na botante (28% increase) sa panahon ng pandemiya pa, para makatala ng di-kapani-paniwalang 65,745,529 na rehistradong boboto para sa 2022 Halalan.

Ngunit sa kabila ng pagyurak na ito sa kaluluwa ng demokrasya, WALA KAMING NARINIG NI ISANG PAGTUTOL MULA SA INYO. Wala kayong nagawa ni isang paghiling sa COMELEC na magtrabaho ng may wagas na KATAPATAN o ang suportahan ang KARAPATAN ng bawat Pilipino ayon sa Saligang Batas para sa Totoong Impormasyon na may pampublikong pakinabang, na siyang ipinaglalaban ng TNTrio sa Korte Suprema para sa taumbayan. Ayon kay Martin Luther King Jr., "Darating ang panahon na ang pananahimik ay mismong pagkakanulo."

Bakit ninyo kami pinabayaan? Bakit ninyo kami iniwan mag-isa sa digmaan, KAYO na mga kababayang pinaniwalaan namin ang integridad at tapang bilang mga pinuno at lingkod-bayan?

Hinihintay naming ang inyong taos-pusong suporta sa labang ito! Umaasa kaming pakikinggan ninyo ang aming hiling!

APPEAL TO THE CURRENT ADMINISTRATION

Kayo ay nailuklok sa kapangyarihan na ang mensahe ay pagkakaisa. Gayunpaman, ang pagkakaisa ay ating makakamtan lamang kung lahat tayo ay napapailalim sa iisang batas na nakabatay sa katotohanan at katarungan. Hindi alintana ang mga pagkakaiba sa mga pang-mundong pananaw at ideolohiya, lahat tayo ay kinakailangang sumunod sa batas.

Ang batas ang nagpo-protekta ng ating mga saligang karapatang-pantao, at ang isa sa mga ito ay ang karapatan sa katotohanan at katapatan ng ating halalan, na siyang simbolo ng ating demokrasya. Ngunit ang legalidad ng inyong administrasyon ay nalalagay sa alanganin dahil may mga ebidensiyang nagpapahiwatig na may pandaraya sa halalan.

Sana ay mapagtanto ninyo na makakapamuno kayo ng mas epektibo kung ang mga pag-aalinlangan ng sambayanan sa legalidad ng inyong administrasyon ay tuluyan nang maiwaksi. Hindi lang ito magiging tagumpay ninyo, ito man ay magiging tagumpay ng demokrasya. Ito ay tunay na makabubuti para sa bansa na mapamahalaan ng isang gobyerno na marangal na kinikilala ng lahat ng kanyang mamamayan.

Nananawagan kami sa inyo na samahan kami sa aming krusada para sa katotohanan, sa pagsuporta sa Writ of Mandamus Petition, na ngayon ay nakahain sa Korte Suprema, pati na ang lumalawak na hiling ng taumbayan upang mapilitan ang COMELEC na ilabas ang mga transmission logs, na siyang makapagpapatunay na ang 2022 Halalan ay patas at malinis, at tunay na sinasalamin ang kalooban ng mga botante.

Kami ay nananawagan sa inyo na himukin ang COMELEC na maging matapat at malinaw at kusang ilabas ang mga impormasyon na lulutas sa nagniningas nang kontrobersiya, ngayon na at para sa ikabubuti ng lahat.

APPEAL TO THE CBCP: THE CALL TO CONSCIENCE

Ang Simbahan ay may napaka-importanteng tungkulin na dapat gampanan bilang konsensiya ng isang bansa. Noong 1986 EDSA People Power Revolution, ang CBCP ang nanindigan at nanguna sa harapan ng rebolusyon, bilang kaisa-isang institusyon na may kakayahang tutulan ang diktadurya ni Marcos Sr., at pakilusin ang taumbayan upang ipaglaban ang kanilang kalayaan. Ipinahayag ng CBCP na ang administrasyon ni Marcos ay nawalan na ng karapatang moral na mamuno dahil sa lantarang pandaraya at panlilinlang.

Kami ay nananawagan ulit sa CBCP na muling gisingin ang natulog na konsensiya ng taumbayan. Ang U.N. International Observer Mission ay idineklara na ang Halalan 2022 ay binigo ang Sambayanang Pilipino, at sina Marcos at Duterte ay nailuklok sa hindi lehitimong paraan. Ang pagsusuri ng TNTrio sa mga resulta ng halalan at sa imposibleng vote ratio na hindi nagbabago sa pagitan ng mga kandidato, ang nag-kumpirma at nag-patunay na may tuwirang dayaan sa halalang ito, suportado ng mga dokumentadong ebidensiya ng pandaraya.

Kami ay natutuwa at pinupuri ang ginagawang pakikipagtulungan ng CBCP sa TNTrio, at sa pagtuturo at pagmumulat sa kaisipan ng mga anak ng Diyos sa pamamagitan ng Basic Ecclesial Communities (BECs) tungkol sa Halalan 2022 at ang napakahalagang pangangailangan na mabago ang kulturang politikal ng bansa.

Utos ng Salita ng Diyos at ayon na rin sa Katolikong pagtuturong panlipunan na ang CBCP ay may moral na obligasyon sa paghanap ng Katotohanan at Hustisya kaugnay sa Halalan 2022. Hiling naming na sana ay maglabas ang CBCP ng Official Statement upang himukin ang COMELEC at lahat ng mga pambansang opisyales na kumilos ng maagap, matapat at malinaw, upang bigyang-daan ang hinihiling ng taumbayan na malaman ang buong katotohanan tungkol sa kaduda-dudang resulta ng Mayo 2022 Halalan.

Bilang aming mga Pastol, tinitingala naming ang CBCP para sa moral na pagpatnubay at pamumuno ngayong panahon ng kawalan ng kasiguruhan, at ang aming tala sa hilaga ay nagdidilim, at ang lahat ay mukhang mawawalan na ng saysay.

APPEAL TO FAITH-BASED COMMUNITIES

Ang relihiyon ay may angking malakas ng impluwensiya sa politika, sa paghubog ng mga panlipunang birtud na pagiging-pamayanan, pagkakaisa at pag-asa. Kahit ano pa mang pagkakaiba ng paniniwala, sistemang etikal at spirituwal na gawi, lahat ng mga komunidad batay sa pananampalataya ay nakikibahagi sa paghanap ng katotohanan at hustisya.

Nananawagan kami sa lahat ng mga Pilipinong kaanib sa iba't-ibang relihiyon, na isabuhay ninyo ang inyong pananampalataya sa pamamagitan ng paglaban para sa katotohanan at katapatan sa Halalan 2022. Ang ating pag-ibig sa Diyos at sa kapwa ay dapat maihayag sa ating mga panlipunan at politikal na pakikipag-ugnayan, dahil ang paghanap ng hustisya ay isang importanteng bahagi ng pananampalataya.

Ang mga mananampalataya sa mga simbahan, templo at mga mosque ay dapat kumilos para sa kabutihan ng lahat at sa pagbabago ng lipunan. Pinapayuhan naming kayo na maging mga emisaryo ng hustisya at pag-asa para sa isang bansang pilay, watak-watak at inabuso.

Nang maharap tayo sa isang pambansang krisis noong 1986, ang mga Pilipino ay lumingon at bumalik sa kanilang pananampalataya upang maipanalo ang rebolusyon na wala ni isang balang pinutok. Sana itong pananampalatayang ito pa rin ang pumatnubay sa ating bansang nasa isang krisis muli, at dalhin tayo sa isang kinabukasang puno ng pag-asa.

Sinasamo namin na lahat ng mga komunidad batay sa pananampalataya ay magka-isa bilang magkaka-tuwang sa ating sama-samang pagsusumikap para sa katotohanan at hustisya.

APPEAL TO THE MILITARY

Ang mga kasundaluhan at kapulisan ay may tungkulin ayon sa Saligang Batas na pagsilbihan, protektahan at ipagtanggol ang Sambayanang Pilipino, pinatnubayan ng mahalagang pag-uugali na tungkulin muna, karangalan at integridad. Ang kamakailang mga kaganapan sa bansa ay binibigyang-diin ang importansiya na paalalahanan ang kasundaluhan at kapulisan sa kanilang responsibilidad sa taumbayan.

Tunay na mahalagang magampanan ng ating mga uniformed personnel ang tungkuling protektahan ang soberanong kalooban ng mga Pilipino sa pagpili ng mga mamumuno sa ating bansa. Ang pagka-sagrado ng balota ay dapat maipatupad at mapanindigan sa lahat ng oras, at walang institusyon, maski na ang COMELEC, ang maaaring mang-maliit sa soberanong kalooban ng taumbayan. Samakatuwid, hinihimok naming ang kasundaluhan at kapulisan na siguraduhin na ang boses ng taumbayan ay dinidinig at ang kanilang mga boto ay nirerespeto at binibilang ng patas at tapat.

At karagdagan pa na kailangan ipaalala sa kanila ay ang tungkulin na isabuhay ang pag-uugali ng may karangalan. Sila ay dapat ginagabayan ng kanilang tungkulin ayon sa Saligang Batas, laban sa tukso ng kayamanan, kapangyarihan o kasikatan, na may nabitag nang karamihan. At sa kanilang pagtindig at pagsaludo sa bandila, sila ay matatawag na mga Tunay na Makabayan, ang kanilang pinaka-marangal na bokasyon at misyon.

Pang-huli, hinihimok naming ang kasundaluhan at kapulisan na panindigan ang paguugali na may integridad, bilang tagapa-tanggol ng taumbayan, sa salita at sa gawa. Panindigan nila ang mga saligang karapatang pantao, partikular ang pangunahing karapatan sa katotohanan at katapatan ng halalan, na siyang kaibuturan ng demokrasya. Sa paninindigan sa mga mahahalagang pag-uugaling ito, mapagsisilbihan ng ating uniformed personnel ang Sambayanang Pilipino at mapo-protektahan ang mga karapatan, upang matiyak ang isang patas at malayang lipunan para sa lahat.

APPEAL TO COLLEGES AND UNIVERSITIES

Ang mga pananaw sa mundo, mga sistemang intelektuwal at mga ideolohiya ay naguunahan sa pagsakop sa mga isip at puso ng ating mga mag-aaral. Ang mga kolehiyo at unibersidad ay mga sentro ng karunungan, kung saan ang mga mag-aaral ay tinuturuang maging mapanuri at malikhain sa pag-iisip, at kayang tahakin ang samu't-saring pananaw sa kanilang paghahanap ng kaalamanan, katotohanan at hustisya.

Hinihimok namin ang mga institusyong akademiko na tuparin ang kanilang misyon na pagkalooban ang mga mag-aaral ng mahalaga at komprehensibong edukasyon na may malawak na saklaw upang makahubog ng mga matatalino't tapat na mga indibidwal na may pag-uugaling moral at espirituwal. Bilang mga taga-hubog ng kabataan, ang mga akademikong institusyon ay ang kuna at pundasyon ng kinabukasan ng ating bansa.

Hinihimok namin sila na sugpuin ang pagpapapalit at pagbabaluktot ng kasaysayan sa kanilang curriculum, na magbubunsod ng maling kaalaman sa kabataang Pilipino, at upang maiwasang magamit ang mga kolehiyo at unibersidad bilang kasangkapan ng mga ideolohiya o panghihikayat, na lalabag sa tunay na kahulugan ng malaya at liberal na edukasyon.

At panghuli, pinapayuhan namin sila na itanim sa katauhan ng ating mga kabataan ang mga mithiin at pagpapahalaga ng ating tradisyon, kasaysayan at kulturang Pilipino, nang sa gayong maipagmamalaki nila ang pamana ng lahi, asamin nilang maging mga tunay na Makabayan, na maninindigan para sa katotohanan, katapatan at hustisya, at maka-buo ng isang patas na lipunang Pilipino, na pahahalagahan ang pangangailangan ng mga dukha at mahihina.

APPEAL TO THE FILIPINO YOUTH

Ang mga Pilipino ngayong nasa edad na 60's hanggang 80's ay mga naging 'frontliners' noon sa laban para sa demokrasya at hustisyang panlipunan. Maski pagod na sila sa mga laban sa personal na buhay at laban para sa bansa, sila ay tuloy pa rin sa paninindigan sa abot ng kanilang lakas at determinasyon.

Ngunit nasaan na ang Kabataang Pilipino?

Nasaan na kayo sa laban para sa Katotohanan, Katapatan at Karapatan para sa Impormasyon na sinusulong ng TNTrio? Ang kabataan noon ang puwersang nagtulak sa First Quarter Storm laban sa rehimeng Marcos, at ang kabataan ngayon ang masiglang enerhiya ng Pink Revolution, na nagbunsod ng espirito ng bolunterismo na ngayon lang nasaksihan sa larangan ng politika. Sa kanilang pag-awit at pag-sayaw sa mensaheng "gobyernong tapat, angat buhay lahat," kanilang kinatawan ang kinabukasan at pag-asa ng bansa.

Nakapanghihinayang na ang mga sandaling iyon ay panandalian lamang, dahil ang kanilang pagsinta at sigla ay naglaho parang bula. Ang resulta ng halalan ang malamang nakapag-pahina ng kanilang kalooban, at sila'y nagsibalik sa kani-kanilang mundo, pinutol ang kanilang pakialam sa mga pambansang suliranin. Iniwan nila ang lipunan na may malaking uka, na sila lamang ang makakapuno.

Nagsusumamo kami sa Kabataang Pilipino na kayo ay tumindig muli mula sa pagkakasadlak at bumalik sa laban. May mga digmaan pa tayong haharapin at tagumpay na kakamtin! Sinasamo naming kayo na samahan ang CBCP at ang lahat ng mga Pilipinong nagmamahal sa demokrasya, at suportahan ang pinaglalaban ng TNTrio, suportahan ang Mandamus Petition na nakasalang sa Korte Suprema, pirmahan ang People's Mandamus (Online) Petition, isumpa ang pandaraya noong Halalan 2022, at habulin ang COMELEC sa kanilang pananagutan.

Maging matatag ang inyong kalooban dahil ang laban na ito ay mahirap at maaaring magtagal. KAYO, na ang mga ninuno ay sina Rizal, Bonifacio at Mabini, ay tinatawagang maging mga Makabayan at mga Bayani. Ilabas ninyo muli ang inyong sigla at pagsinta upang mapagningas ang kilusan at maipaglaban ang kaluluwa ng ating demokrasya. Kinabukasan ninyo ang nakataya ngayon. Hindi ba nararapat na kasama namin KAYO sa laban na ito?

APPEAL TO THE WHISTLEBLOWERS

Ang pandaraya, lalo na ang sistematiko at malawakang pandaraya, ay hindi ginagawang mag-isa. Sa isang sulok, may ilang tao na naging bahagi ng pakana na dayain ang eleksyon ang nagkukulong at nagtatago ng katotohanan sa mata ng sambayanan.

Dapat ilantad sa liwanag ang isang krimeng ginawa sa dilim laban sa sambayanang Pilipino. Ang tagong pandaraya ay dapat ibunyag. Hindi matatahimik sa kanilang budhi ang mga "whistleblower" at mga saksi sa ganitong krimen at kasinungalingan. Kung kikipkipin nito hanggang sa huli, hindi sila mapapanatag kahit sa kanilang libingan.

Pakiusap, sa ngalan ng dangal na kaloob ng Diyos at ng inyong pagmamahal sa bayan, at sa inyong mga mahal sa buhay, at alang-alang din sa kapayapaan ng inyong kalooban, lumantad na kayo at manindigan. Hanggang kailan ninyo maitatago ang hawak ninyong katotohanan, kapag sumobra na ang bigat at hindi na makayanan?

Maging budhi ng ating bayan! Magpakabayani! Magsalita na! Ang inyong salita ang magiging buhay ng ating bansâ, ang inyong buhay ay magiging pag-asa ng bayan. Kahit dito man lang sa isang pasya ng kagitingan, magkakaroon ng malalim na kahulugan ang inyong buhay.

PLEASE SHARE THIS POST. Please sign the People's Mandamus to pressure SC to compel Comelec to release the transmission logs.

SIGNED BY:

List of Signatories

....

12
ESP by Franklins Ysaac – May 30, 2023

In our private lives, we make decisions about our future .

Call it ESP or extra sensory power which we alll have but experience, knowledge and beliefs all contribute to our ability to predict our future.

You don't have to see a fortune teller because that's his way of surviving . You are gifted anyway with the special talent God gave you .

Sometimes, amongst my family members, I envy my brother who is an artist, a musician , a composer, a philosopher, a teacher all rolled into one . But he said he wanted to exchange his talent for my talent as finance wizard . He wants to make quick money the way I tell him about my banking experience.

No, you cannot exchange your special talent for another's special talent .

Be satisfied with your special talent and make it work for you .

Talents also grow as we mature and age . Sometimes we find our work boring and we want to try other talents .

Well, you can start with a hobby then develop into business by learning from other businessmen and entrepreneurs.

But don't, don't imitate or copy from others as this may not turn out to be good for you .

Perhaps, instincts work too. If you don't feel good about an idea, drop it.

And don't borrow money to do a startup. Use OPM or other people's money but spend time with your business and don't let others run the business for you .

Now, what are we doing with our comelec campaign for truth ? We all know they are hiding the truth even after we have exposed them. Ayaw pa aminin! Huli na nga gusto pa lumaban !

When we started this campaign, we already knew the election was a farce. A set up which at the first hour, there was massive cheating. We stuck with our theories and in the end the theories proved to be true.

So, we went legal and still in denial pa rin sila .

How is this going to end ?

I predict that heads will roll and something good will turn out after they have been cornered. There's going to be no way out. We gave them all the chances to give us what we own and that is the truth .

We won't pay them for this but it has cost us legal fees . But no matter what happens, we will all be vindicated and personally I could see good things happening again like a feeling of euphoria after the 1986 peaceful revolution .

That's my prediction . Dare sayeth not regulators !

....

13

Posted by Fanklin Ysaac – June 1, 2023 – Jarius Bondoc Column – Avoid Paying Taxes

Sharing the civil disobedience campaign which I raised already .

No taxes, no monies for this bankrupt and corrupt government !

Avoid paying taxes once

Maharlika steals our pensions

by Jarius Bondoc – June 2, 2023

Our pension, health and housing contributions are in peril. This, after Malacañang and Congress railroaded passage of the Maharlika Investment Fund.

They pretended to heed public outcry. At first, they excluded from capitalizing Maharlika with our SSS, GSIS, PhilHealth, Pag-Ibig, OWWA and PVAO. But by slyly including the words "may" and "option", they will still take our money.

Their greed is insatiable. In the Legislature they steal hundred-billion-peso flood control and roadwork funds. In the Executive they pocket procurement kickbacks and confidential-intelligence funds.

Now they will take even our hard-earned cash for healthcare, homebuying, college, retirement, burial and emergencies. After all, it's they who appoint administrators of our fund contributions.

Last November the House of Reps hastily enacted Maharlika for President Ferdinand Marcos Jr.'s trip to Davos. Last Wednesday, May 31, the Senate rushed its version for Marcos Jr.'s second State of the Nation.

But Maharlika is not just for presidential vanity. It is, as objectors warn, for "crony capitalism".

Critics coined that term during the dictatorship of Marcos Jr.'s father. Marcos Sr. granted behest loans to golfing buddies from government-run pensions and - owned banks PNB, DBP, Landbank.

Those loans supposedly were to benefit Filipinos through industrial investments. The First Couple and cronies instead divvied up the cash to amass castles, mansions, ranches, private jets, limos, art masterpieces, jewelry, fur coats and 3,000 pairs of shoes.

A Malaysian politico recently was caught pillaging the One MDB sovereign fund. Prime Minister Najib Razak and wife are in prison for absconding with $1.25 billion. Stashed in their manor were suitcases of cash, jewelry, fur coats, wristwatches, signature bags and shoes.

Philippine courts have regained P174 billion Marcos Sr. loot. Still to be recovered is P125 billion. Eerily that missing amount is the same Maharlika initial capital to be taken from DBP, Landbank, Bangko Sentral. It's equivalent to $2.5 billion, double the 1MDB hoard.

Marcos Jr. will sit as or appoint the Maharlika chairman. He will pick the directors, advisers, managers. If they plunder Maharlika they won't go to jail. Their Maharlika law metes only P5-million fine. A drop in the P125-billion bucket.

Businessmen, laborers, academics, activists, church and civic leaders united against Maharlika. The political elite crushed their dissent.

Who concocted Maharlika? Marcos Jr. never mentioned it in his election campaign, nor in his first State of the Nation, nor in his Medium-Term Fiscal Framework. Thus, the suspicions about the intent: plunder, money laundering.

Genuine sovereign funds like Norway's and Singapore's are reeling from global inflation. Though untimely, our rulers forced Maharlika through. They plan to invest it abroad; in the same breath they invite foreign investors. They say Maharlika will earn from rural roads and bridges, but who makes money out of those?

Some beg Marcos Jr. to veto onerous Maharlika law provisos. Others are to question it at the Supreme Court. A few are forming watchdog groups. Most are resigned to having our pensions and contributions raided.

But we're not exactly helpless. There's a way to starve political leeches of blood to suck. Let's avoid paying taxes.

How? Barter goods and services. Buy from low-income earners who need not issue official receipts.

Make family purchases via our VAT-exempt seniors and persons with disabilities. Avail of all possible income-tax deductions for dependence and expenses. Postpone tax payments till the last minute.

When touring, book untaxed homestays, hostels, pension lodges. Buy from roadside hawkers.

Avail of all possible loans and benefits from SSS, GSIS, PhilHealth, Pag-Ibig, OWWA, PVAO. Postpone repayments till absolute deadline. Collect matured 20-year contributions from Pag-Ibig.

Shun admin fundraisers. Boycott crony-capitalist businesses.

Emigrate, and announce that it's in disgust with kleptocrats.

All these are legal – unlike what they're doing to us.

* * *

Catch Sapol radio show, Saturdays, 8 to 10 a.m., DWIZ (882-AM).

14

Top IT Experts Seek Probe of 2022 Election Results

+Eliseo Rio Jr + Gus Lagman

PRESS RELEASE

Top IT experts seek probe of 2022 election results

QUEZON CITY, PHILIPPINES – Three experts in the field of information technology (IT) have called for an investigation into allegations of irregularities during the recent national elections., The panel of IT experts was composed of Eliseo Rio Jr., Augusto Lagman, and Franklin Ysaac at the "Pandesal Forum" in Kamuning Bakery Café today.

Lagman is currently the Chairman of the National Citizens' Movement for Free Elections (NAMFREL) and was formerly a Commissioner of the Commission on Elections (COMELEC). He also had management stints at IBM Philippines, Logic Management Inc., and the Automobile Association of the Philippines.

According to the NAMFREL National Chairman, "the law authorizes the COMELEC to use an automated election system that encourages transparency, credibility, fairness, and accuracy of elections and that reflects the genuine will of the people. The present COMELEC system, while fast, does not meet the transparency requirement, mainly because precinct-counting is automated and therefore not witnessed nor understood by the voters. To correct this, COMELEC should shift to the hybrid system that entails manual precinct-counting (for transparency) and automated canvassing (for speed)."

Rio served as Acting Secretary of the Department of Information and Communications Technology (DICT) and Commissioner of the National Telecommunications Commission (NTC). A retired general in the Armed Forces of the Philippines (AFP), he was the AFP Deputy Chief of Staff for Communications, Electronics, and Information Systems.

The erstwhile DICT and NTC chief said: "The 2022 election results that came out from the COMELEC Transparency Server from 7:17pm, May 9 to 3:18pm, May 13 were published in media for the public to see. It was noticed that a distinct pattern emerged such that one can actually predict, with very small margin of error, the number of votes of each and every major candidate for President and VP in the new updates by just knowing the votes that the front runners got and the vote ratio of the last update. This pattern can in fact be put in a simple linear equation, and this is statistically improbable with random events."

Ysaac was a former President of the Financial Executives Institute of the Philippines (FINEX) who served as Chairman of FINEX Research and Development Foundation. A retired banker, he ventured into software development and has developed electronic operating systems for the banking industry, where he used to be an executive in Citibank and two other banks.

The banker-turned-IT-entrepreneur believes that "for transparency, the COMELEC should allow an independent audit body composed of IT professionals to review the program, to conduct a review of all secure data (SD) cards which contain the program prior to installation in all vote counting machines (VCMs), and to audit the same SD cards immediately after the election prior to transmission of election returns to the COMELEC'S central, back-up, and transparency servers. If there are discrepancies found, said VCMs should be opened and the SD cards should be rechecked while the counting should be done manually."

Media Contact:
KKK Para Sa Bayan
katipunan.parasabayan@gmail.com

15
Comelec Issue is a Grave Issue
– Oswaldo Magno –
June 7, 2023

The TNTrio's allegation of election rigging regarding the May 9 elections, about which there exist palpable direct as well as circumstantial evidence (including the COMELEC Transparency Servers counting results ahead of VCM transmissions, change or alteration of earlier presented data by COMELEC) is a very grave issue. We hope that the Supreme Court will not unduly delay its decision on the Mandamus case or come up with a ruling that will only serve to anger the people and provoke civil unrest or even another people power.

Panawagan sa Supreme Court

Ang may patunay na pagmanipula ng resulta ng halalan noong Mayo 9 ay isang napakabigat na isyu. Sana ay hindi kayo maglalabas ng desisyon na magdudulot lamang ng galit sa sambayanang Pilipino at mag-uudyok ng kaguluhan sibil o panibagong people power.

Manawagan tayo, Bayan 

....

16
Sharing this paper written by the experts from UP School of Economics.- Franklin Ysaac – June 7, 2023

Their colleagues who now head and work for this corrupt govt think and believe otherwise.

What a shame ! They should be ostracized and not allowed to set foot in the UP economics classes . Not even a teaching position should be granted these destroyers of our economy after they leave the government .

………………

📣New Discussion Paper

📄 Title: Maharlika Investment Fund: Still Beyond Repair

📝Authors: Ma. Joy V. Abrenica, PhD; Luzeta C. Adorna, PhD; Patricia T. Coseteng; Emmanuel S. de Dios, PhD; Marian S. de los Angeles, PhD; Noel B. Del Castillo; Benjamin A. Endriga; Laarni C. Escresa, PhD; Jonna P. Estudillo, PhD; Maria Socorro Gochoco-Bautista, PhD; Aleli D. Kraft, PhD; Alice A. Lee; Adrian R. Mendoza, PhD; Ernesto M. Pernia, PhD; Jan Carlo B. Punongbayan, PhD; Renato E. Reside Jr., PhD; Anthony G. Sabarillo, PhD; Orville Jose C. Solon, PhD; Gerard P. Suanes; Elizabeth Tan; Atty. Mariel Jances Nhayin P. Yamashita

Abstract: The administration of President Ferdinand Marcos Jr. is pushing for the creation of the Maharlika Investment Fund (MIF). Originally proposed as a sovereign wealth fund, the MIF later on morphed into what can be called a sovereign investment fund (SIF): a state-owned investment fund that aims to reap returns from financial investments as well as economic returns from developmental projects like infrastructure. We find that the MIF violates fundamental principles of economics and finance and poses serious risks to the economy and the public sector — notwithstanding its proponents' good intentions.

• First, the raison d'être of the Maharlika Investment Fund remains unclear even as it has already hurdled both houses of Congress.

• Second, due to its confused goals, the MIF bill does not adequately articulate and take account of several implications of the fund's dual-bottom line objective.

• Third, the manner of funding the Maharlika Investment Fund poses huge risks to our already strained public coffers and is vulnerable to moral hazard.

• Fourth, red flags abound in the MIC's governance structure.

• Fifth, with elevated global economic headwinds and uncertainties, it is unlikely that MIF will be able to "crowd-in" investments and eke out returns that are large enough for the fund to grow substantially to finance development projects.

• Sixth, the preoccupation with this defective proposal has diverted attention from more vital and urgent national agenda that the administration itself has rightly identified, notably the need to reform the retirement and pension system for military and uniformed personnel.

In view of the foregoing, we call upon President Marcos to seriously reconsider the final approval of the Maharlika Investment Fund bill, and present before the public a clear and solid rationale for setting it up in the first place. We also call on our former and present colleagues who are now part of the Marcos economic team to reconsider their position on Maharlika and advise the President accordingly, in line with their best appreciation of their discipline and the reservations expressed by the rest of the economics profession of the country.

📌Read the full paper here:

https://econ.upd.edu.ph/.../ind.../dp/article/view/155 1/1035

....

17
APPEAL TO WHISTLEBLOWERS –
Tina A. Astorga – June 7, 2023

Fraud, especially fraud that is systematic and far reaching, cannot be done by a single person. Somewhere, someone who has been part of the scheme of this election deceit could be hiding and holding the truth from our people.

A crime committed against the Filipino people in the dark must be brought to light. A lie hidden in the secrecy of deceit must be exposed. Whistleblowers who know of this crime, and are a witness to this lie, cannot bear them on their conscience for long. If they bring these to their grave, even there they would not find peace.

We appeal, in the name of your God-given dignity and of your love for our people, and for your family, and for the sake of your peace, come out and take a stand. How long would you be able to hide the truth you know, when the burden of truth is too heavy for one to carry?

Be the conscience of our nation. Take the heroic act. Speak! Your word shall be the nation's life, your truth shall be the nation's hope. If only for this one noble act of courage, your life shall find an ultimate meaning.

PLEASE SHARE!
SIGNED BY:
List of Signatories.
Filipino Translation:
APPEAL TO THE WHISTLEBLOWERS

Ang pandaraya, lalo na ang sistematiko at malawakang pandaraya, ay hindi ginagawang mag-isa. Sa isang sulok, may ilang tao na naging bahagi ng pakana na dayain ang eleksyon ang nagkukulong at nagtatago ng katotohanan sa mata ng sambayanan.

Dapat ilantad sa liwanag ang isang krimeng ginawa sa dilim laban sa sambayanang Pilipino. Ang tagong pandaraya ay dapat ibunyag. Hindi matatahimik sa kanilang budhi ang mga "whistleblower" at mga saksi sa ganitong krimen at kasinungalingan. Kung kikipkipin nito hanggang sa huli, hindi sila mapapanatag kahit sa kanilang libingan.

Pakiusap, sa ngalan ng dangal na kaloob ng Diyos at ng inyong pagmamahal sa bayan, at sa inyong mga mahal sa buhay, at alang-alang din sa kapayapaan ng inyong kalooban, lumantad na kayo at manindigan. Hanggang kailan ninyo maitatago ang hawak ninyong katotohanan, kapag sumobra na ang bigat at hindi na makayanan?

Maging budhi ng ating bayan! Magpakabayani! Magsalita na! Ang inyong salita ang magiging buhay ng ating bansâ, ang inyong buhay ay magiging pag-asa ng bayan. Kahit dito man lang sa isang pasya ng kagitingan, magkakaroon ng malalim na kahulugan ang iyong buhay

....

18

Rigged Philippines 2022 Elections

PLEASE SHARE this message delivered in New York City during the Philippine Independence Day Parade on June 4, 2023. – Mila Alvarez Magno posted this

"Rigged Philippine 2022 Elections"
Friends,

Today, I am compelled to bring to your attention a grave injustice suffered by the Filipino people in the May 9, 2022, National Elections.

It is an injustice that all Filipinos, wherever they live, must unite in solidarity to correct.

As most of you know, the May 9 National Elections were not in any way a fair, free, and honest election.

We witnessed a shocking anomaly—an unprecedented vote count of 20 million votes, mostly for Marcos Jr. and Sara Duterte, in less than 1 hour after the polls closed. In just two hours after the polls closed, Marcos Jr. and Duterte claimed the highest executive positions by millions of votes.

This was the finding of three men who are intimately familiar with electoral systems and electoral processes and are now known by their monicker, TNTrio, or Truth and Transparency Trio.

Independently of the TNTrio, an International Observer Mission in their final report noted the presence of massive vote buying, disenfranchisement, disinformation, and even violence. Their report concluded that Marcos Jr. and Sara Duterte were not elected legitimately.

How could 20 million votes be transmitted in one hour in a country with slow and unreliable internet? Why did the BBM versus Leni ratio remain constant in all precincts, regardless of regional preferences?

How did BBM receive more votes than the top senator? Why did voter registration increase by 27% during COVID lockdowns when historical growth is only 1-3% annually?

And why did COMELEC's Transparency Servers count votes before the Election Results were transmitted by the Vote Counting Machines? There is concrete evidence, such as printed election return receipts, that supports the claim that COMELEC's Transparency Servers reported results prior to the transmission of data by the VCMs.

Based on the data that came from COMELEC itself, including what COMELEC deceptively claimed to be Transmission Logs and posted on its website on March 23, 2023, there is direct evidence of election fraud. THEY ALL POINT TO THE FACT THAT THE ELECTION WAS RIGGED!

There is now pending in the Supreme Court a legal action called Mandamus which was filed by the TNTrio in November of last year.

The Mandamus Petition seeks an Order directing COMELEC to preserve and to make available evidence, in the form of Transmission Logs, to prove that the 20M votes reported by COMELEC in the first hour of vote counting are valid.

However, the Supreme Court has been slow to act.

The COMELEC failed to be transparent and honest about the staggering 20M votes by altering the data it initially presented on October 19, 2022, before the Mandamus Petition was filed. In a forum at Ateneo University, the COMELEC reported that VCM transmissions reached their highest point at the end of the second hour. However, in the logs posted on the COMELEC website on March 23, 2023, they changed their statement, now claiming that VCM transmissions peaked at the end of the first hour.

Not only that, COMELEC is now saying that VCM transmissions started at 7:08 pm, instead of the 7:19 pm start date that it had previously reported in October last year.

What can we conclude from these alterations? COMELEC IS CHANGING THE DATA TO FIT THE FALSE NARRATIVE THAT THE 20M VOTES IT REPORTED IN THE FIRST HOUR ON MAY 9 ARE LEGITIMATE!

Friends, we cannot and we should not allow this travesty to go uncorrected. We must hold those responsible for rigging the elections accountable!

All of us, together, must exert pressure on both the COMELEC and the Supreme Court to address the palpable evidence of election fraud in a transparent and forthright manner!

The legal battle being waged by the TNTrio in the Supreme Court is the legal battle of our lifetimes. It is a battle for the TRUTH, TRANSPARENCY and our RIGHT TO INFORMATION. There is nothing more important and consequential to the future of our democracy and our country. It is extremely worthy of our support.

There is an online petition on the https://chng.it/Yyv7gHPtYJ website that you, your family and friends, can sign as a show of support for the TNTrio's fight against COMELEC. It's called the People's Mandamus. The online petition as of today has over 38,000 signatures. Let us help bring the number of signatories to 1 MILLION!

By signing the online petition, we show solidarity with the TNTrio in their fight. We demand the truth and want COMELEC to know that we stand with them. We also call on the Supreme Court to quickly intervene and instruct COMELEC to release authentic transmission logs for verifying the contested election results.

There is also a fundraising campaign on the GoFundMe website (https://bit.ly/GFMTNTRIO) to raise funds to help defray the legal costs of the Mandamus legal action. I urge all of you who are able to contribute to the Legal Fund after you get home today.

An Open Letter has been sent to past and present high-profile politicians, urging them to support the fight for truth, transparency, and citizens' right to information. The letter has been shared on social media, along with a link for you to add your name as a signatory. Please consider adding your name to the Open Letter (https://bit.ly/OrgSupportMandamus). Your participation adds weight to the call for action, which politicians would be unwise to ignore.

So, friends, I end this speech with these words: PARTICIPATE IN THE FIGHT FOR TRUTH, TRANSPARENCY, AND RIGHT TO INFORMATION. ACTIVELY FIGHT FOR THE BETTERMENT OF OUR BELOVED PHILIPPINES. LET US UNITE AND MAKE OUR VOICES HEARD. TOGETHER, WE CAN MAKE A DIFFERENCE AND CONTRIBUTE TO OUR NATION'S PROGRESS.

https://www.facebook.com/mila.alvarez.magno/posts/6172221216228797

....

19
Comelec Deleted Back Up Files – Franklin Ysaac – June 9, 2023

This news reached us and there have been messages of concern regarding this back up files being deleted or destroyed .

Those are back up files but what they can't destroy are your ballots in the boxes which we will compel Comelec to open and count manually all ballots and compare them with SD cards.

We already found truth in certain precincts in Pangasinan where actual votes of one candidate did not match with smartmatic result .

We have proven somebody manipulated and programmed the SS cards to come out with desired equation favoring one candidate .

So no worries po tayo. Alive na alive pa po petition natin.

Ignore this news of Comelec deletion of back up files .

INQUIRER.net
INQUIRER.NET
LATEST NEWS STORIES
Comelec deletes backup files used in May 9 polls
BY DANIZA FERNANDEZ | INQUIRER.NET
JUNE 15, 2022 AT 11:09 AM • 1 MIN READ
MANILA, Philippines — The Commission on Elections
COMMISSION ON ELECTIONS
REPUBLIC OF THE PHILIPPINES

20

Transparency, Corruption and Mass Poverty – Oswal Magno – June 10, 2023

LET'S UNDERSTAND THE CONNECTION BETWEEN LACK OF TRANSPARENCY, CORRUPTION AND MASS POVERTY.

LET'S UNDERSTAND THE CONNECTION BETWEEN SHADOW GOVERNMENT, CORRUPTION AND WIDE POVERTY

The Mandamus case now pending in the Supreme Court is truly an unprecedented case. There has never been a case like it. A favorable decision will be a big win for transparency in governance. Organizations like Transparency International and others recognize that lack of transparency in governance fosters abuse of power and lack of accountability, which in turn are responsible for systemic corruption that takes away resources needed for social and economic development. If the governance is transparent, the corruption that is the cause of widespread poverty in our country will be reduced or eliminated. So let's support TNTrio's fight for truth and transparent governance.

> *Bakit mahalaga ang Maaninag na Pamamahala*
>
> **Ang ugat ng kurapsyon ay hindi maaninag na pamamahala. Kung walang kurapsyon, tiyak lalago ang ating ekonomya at marami sa atin hindi na kailangan magpunta sa ibat-ibang bansa para magpa-alila at mapalayo sa kanilang mga mahal sa buhay.**
>
> Ipaglaban ang "Transparency" Bayan! 

....

21
2022 Elections has proofs of tampering – Eliseo Rios jr – posted by Danny Yap – June 13, 2023

The Commission on Elections (COMELEC) and its Automated Election System provider Smartmatic, have made a change in their protocols, which prevented the tracing of the actual source of transmission of votes from precincts that can potentially be used to tamper with the results as warned by then Senate President Tito Sotto and Senator Ping Lacson.

And here are the proofs that the results of the 2022 Election were TAMPERED OR RIGGED, as warned. In the "Raw Files" (gzip) uploaded by COMELEC on their website last March 23, 2023 (updated March 27), these observations were made. In the first hour of counting by the Transparency Server, several precinct Election Returns (ER) received from different VCMs HAVE THE SAME IP ADDRESS!

This can now explain why in the first hour, the Transparency Server (TS) was counting faster than what the VCMs were actually transmitting because the ERs were coming from ONE fabricated source. This can account for the unbelievable 20M+ votes shown to the public on 8:02pm of May 9, 2022. This also explains why the Transparency Server was receiving ERs EVEN BEFORE the precinct VCMs have transmitted them. Whoever manipulated the results of the TS already knew the ERs that the pre-programmed VCMs will be sending.

And the events that led to these irregularities, aside from the change in the transmission protocols were:-

1) The change from the reviewed source code (software) that was downloaded in ALL VCMs discovered by NAMFREL before the 2022 Election, which until now remains unresolved.

2) The configuration of SD cards by COMELEC WITHOUT ANY witnesses as required by law, lamely using Covid-19 protocol as an excuse.

Beyond reasonable doubt, the 2022 Election was RIGGED!

ctto Eliseo Rio Jr

NO. 1-106,023	CLUSTERED	RECEPTION DATETIME	IP ADDRESS
24	55140032	09-May-2022 19:08:53	10.11.25.135
16	13190023	09-May-2022 19:08:53	10.11.60.171
89340	65090049	09-May-2022 23:59:56	10.12.18.108
38	60080001	09-May-2022 19:08:55	10.12.5.168
69	30070009	09-May-2022 19:08:59	10.12.6.190
28	15200003	09-May-2022 19:08:54	10.12.6.244
74	47160006	09-May-2022 19:08:59	10.12.7.20
71	30250060	09-May-2022 19:08:59	10.12.7.30
52	37480028	09-May-2022 19:08:57	10.12.7.39
51	34220028	09-May-2022 19:08:57	10.12.7.46
58	31010077	09-May-2022 19:08:58	10.12.7.51
89330	91010004	09-May-2022 23:59:50	10.19.10.11
62510	90030106	09-May-2022 20:48:22	10.19.11.172
60853	90050001	09-May-2022 20:42:25	10.19.12.202
55	65090069	09-May-2022 19:08:57	10.19.13.185
72358	93150001	09-May-2022 21:39:15	10.19.13.92
67397	91050010	09-May-2022 21:10:06	10.19.14.182
81	31210013	09-May-2022 19:09:00	10.19.19.134
68671	92010050	09-May-2022 21:17:03	10.19.2.23
66347	92040006	09-May-2022 21:04:56	10.19.2.40
65662	93150002	09-May-2022 21:01:44	10.19.2.8
57	26130035	09-May-2022 19:08:58	10.19.3.57
60	37170058	09-May-2022 19:08:58	10.47.2.116
89336	38130025	09-May-2022 23:59:55	10.47.4.22
64	53160187	09-May-2022 19:08:58	10.47.4.32
66	72200042	09-May-2022 19:08:58	10.47.6.101
75	55020033	09-May-2022 19:08:59	10.47.6.107
40	33070011	09-May-2022 19:08:56	10.47.6.128
50	33130017	09-May-2022 19:08:57	10.47.6.129
22	32110005	09-May-2022 19:08:53	10.47.6.132
44	12250029	09-May-2022 19:08:57	10.47.6.215
34	37480057	09-May-2022 19:08:55	10.47.6.58
11	31020042	09-May-2022 19:08:52	10.47.6.96
53	40050067	09-May-2022 19:08:57	10.47.7.30
70	30200031	09-May-2022 19:08:59	10.47.7.50
4	15260038	09-May-2022 19:08:51	10.47.7.58
13	31370080	09-May-2022 19:08:52	10.47.7.60
42	52100007	09-May-2022 19:08:56	10.47.7.66
72	31370028	09-May-2022 19:08:59	10.47.7.67
62	50020030	09-May-2022 19:08:58	10.47.7.8
4646	49240020	09-May-2022 19:18:23	192.168.0.121
2	10050317	09-May-2022 19:08:51	192.168.0.2
77	21040073	09-May-2022 19:09:00	192.168.0.2
158	74040926	09-May-2022 19:09:11	192.168.0.2
403	10330016	09-May-2022 19:10:36	192.168.0.2

NO. 1-106,023	CLUSTERED	RECEPTION DATETIME	IP ADDRESS
490	10170045	09-May-2022 19:11:13	192.168.0.2
564	39071677	09-May-2022 19:11:41	192.168.0.2
633	75010597	09-May-2022 19:12:06	192.168.0.2
645	76050431	09-May-2022 19:12:10	192.168.0.2
673	75010437	09-May-2022 19:12:23	192.168.0.2
708	75010211	09-May-2022 19:12:31	192.168.0.2
710	21110033	09-May-2022 19:12:32	192.168.0.2
737	39020715	09-May-2022 19:12:36	192.168.0.2
758	39061052	09-May-2022 19:12:40	192.168.0.2
765	34050372	09-May-2022 19:12:42	192.168.0.2
815	10280020	09-May-2022 19:12:54	192.168.0.2
832	75010044	09-May-2022 19:12:57	192.168.0.2
835	34240120	09-May-2022 19:12:58	192.168.0.2
849	39141524	09-May-2022 19:13:01	192.168.0.2
854	39010420	09-May-2022 19:13:02	192.168.0.2
880	75010802	09-May-2022 19:13:07	192.168.0.2
917	39040683	09-May-2022 19:13:17	192.168.0.2
952	75010034	09-May-2022 19:13:24	192.168.0.2
970	10340021	09-May-2022 19:13:28	192.168.0.2
971	21080235	09-May-2022 19:13:28	192.168.0.2
984	39111301	09-May-2022 19:13:30	192.168.0.2
1000	75010678	09-May-2022 19:13:34	192.168.0.2
1026	74030517	09-May-2022 19:13:39	192.168.0.2
1032	74030505	09-May-2022 19:13:41	192.168.0.2
1036	21080239	09-May-2022 19:13:42	192.168.0.2
1048	21200159	09-May-2022 19:13:44	192.168.0.2
1083	34050432	09-May-2022 19:13:51	192.168.0.2
1085	74030258	09-May-2022 19:13:51	192.168.0.2
1096	75010867	09-May-2022 19:13:53	192.168.0.2
1101	21110038	09-May-2022 19:13:55	192.168.0.2
1104	34050026	09-May-2022 19:13:55	192.168.0.2
1115	10340009	09-May-2022 19:13:57	192.168.0.2
1122	76020435	09-May-2022 19:13:58	192.168.0.2
1123	10130005	09-May-2022 19:13:59	192.168.0.2
1158	74041564	09-May-2022 19:14:06	192.168.0.2
1172	74041736	09-May-2022 19:14:08	192.168.0.2
1178	39010318	09-May-2022 19:14:09	192.168.0.2
1181	21080092	09-May-2022 19:14:10	192.168.0.2
1188	21180074	09-May-2022 19:14:11	192.168.0.2
1206	34050249	09-May-2022 19:14:13	192.168.0.2
1207	39030899	09-May-2022 19:14:13	192.168.0.2
1211	10070020	09-May-2022 19:14:14	192.168.0.2
1212	10220025	09-May-2022 19:14:14	192.168.0.2
1220	75010600	09-May-2022 19:14:15	192.168.0.2
1229	74020350	09-May-2022 19:14:16	192.168.0.2
1230	10160027	09-May-2022 19:14:17	192.168.0.2

7:04

× CLUSTERED# AND IP ADD…

106,023	CLUSTERED	RECEPTION DATETIME	IP ADDRESS
1236	39050873	09-May-2022 19:14:17	192.168.0.2
1257	10340037	09-May-2022 19:14:21	192.168.0.2
1263	74040011	09-May-2022 19:14:23	192.168.0.2
1264	10050065	09-May-2022 19:14:24	192.168.0.2
1293	39061050	09-May-2022 19:14:28	192.168.0.2
1308	75040520	09-May-2022 19:14:30	192.168.0.2
1319	39050875	09-May-2022 19:14:32	192.168.0.2
1320	39101337	09-May-2022 19:14:32	192.168.0.2
1329	39141827	09-May-2022 19:14:33	192.168.0.2
1334	74010147	09-May-2022 19:14:33	192.168.0.2
1335	74040821	09-May-2022 19:14:33	192.168.0.2
1342	10100029	09-May-2022 19:14:35	192.168.0.2
1348	76040455	09-May-2022 19:14:35	192.168.0.2
1479	21190080	09-May-2022 19:14:53	192.168.0.2
1758	76030309	09-May-2022 19:15:28	192.168.0.2
1787	10310046	09-May-2022 19:15:32	192.168.0.2
1833	74030610	09-May-2022 19:15:37	192.168.0.2
1834	10140320	09-May-2022 19:15:38	192.168.0.2
1846	75010251	09-May-2022 19:15:38	192.168.0.2
1852	74050010	09-May-2022 19:15:39	192.168.0.2
1853	10310157	09-May-2022 19:15:40	192.168.0.2
1863	74041029	09-May-2022 19:15:40	192.168.0.2
1864	75010736	09-May-2022 19:15:40	192.168.0.2
1869	39010432	09-May-2022 19:15:41	192.168.0.2
1872	74040046	09-May-2022 19:15:41	192.168.0.2
1893	39101374	09-May-2022 19:15:43	192.168.0.2
1896	75010885	09-May-2022 19:15:43	192.168.0.2
1904	75010875	09-May-2022 19:15:44	192.168.0.2
1905	10340045	09-May-2022 19:15:45	192.168.0.2
1913	74041783	09-May-2022 19:15:45	192.168.0.2
1914	75040380	09-May-2022 19:15:45	192.168.0.2
1915	76040253	09-May-2022 19:15:45	192.168.0.2
1924	21060480	09-May-2022 19:15:47	192.168.0.2
1928	10080039	09-May-2022 19:15:48	192.168.0.2
1959	10010006	09-May-2022 19:15:51	192.168.0.2
1993	34240016	09-May-2022 19:15:54	192.168.0.2
13835	21150053	09-May-2022 19:24:13	192.168.0.2

....

22
TNTRIO Analysis – June 12, 2023 – Eliseo Rio Jr.

In the first hour of counting after voting closed, the Transparency Server (TS) counted an incredible 20M+ votes, the highest one-hour count in our electoral history, and showed this to public at 8:02pm of May 9, 2022. However, in a public Forum held on October 18, 2022, COMELEC proudly showed a graph which depicted Accumulated VCM Transmissions that PEAKED at the SECOND HOUR, in stark contrast with the Transparency Server count that PEAKED at the FIRST HOUR. In those two hours, from 8pm to 9pm, the TS was counting votes FASTER than what the VCMs were actually transmitting.

Now we know why! In those first two hours, the Transparency Server was RECEIVING Election Returns from some illegal Local Area Networks (LANs) and NOT from actual VCM transmissions. In the "Raw Files" uploaded in the COMELEC website last March 23, 2023 (updated on March 27), it is shown there that PRIVATE IP addresses were used to transmit the ERs. This is illegal because ALL VCM must transmit DIRECTLY to the COMELEC Servers using PUBLIC IP addresses of Telcos, for using a private network could make possible the tampering of ERs hidden from public view. In that same Forum of October 18, Chairman George Garcia committed to make public the Telcos' Transmission Logs. Until now COMELEC has shown only Reception Logs that are full of anomalies and discrepancies.

And in those two hours, "TAPOS NA ANG BOKSING" as to who won the Presidency and VP.

I really think that some IT personnel in COMELEC purposely posted these Raw Files in the COMELEC website to alert the public of the biggest SCAM in our electoral history. They are the virtual whistleblowers, as patriotic as the COMELEC programmers who walked out in the counting of the 1986 snap election. TO YOU WHO POSTED THESE RAW FILES FOR THE PUBLIC TO SEE, A GRATEFUL NATION SALUTES YOU!

....

Oswald Magno

Based on Sir Ely's findings that many VCMs had the same IP address using an illegal private network, it can be deduced that a large portion of the early votes (20M+) counted by the Transparency Server during the first hour are the same as the false or fabricated vote results at the precincts represented by the VCMs. It stands to reason that whoever fed the Transparency Servers with the early votes coming from the private network when most VCMs were not yet ready to transmit already knew what the vote results will be from the VCMs having the same IP address.

....

23
Something new from a friend formerly with government. – Col Leonardo O. Odono – June 13, 2023

If you love your country and stand for the truth, read this without any distraction. Posted as requested for the information and perusal of the readers.

"Comrades and friends,

The truth seekers', our, search for the truth about those 20M votes supposed to have been counted at precinct level and transmitted to the transparency server of Comelec within only one hour after close of the 2022 election, is done.

Comelec refused to release proof of transmission of the questionable 20M votes which I requested in a letter I sent to the poll body, on November 26, 2022 - in the exercise of my constitutional right of access to information of public concern in the hands of a government agency, within the purview of the Freedom of Information regime in the country. It is the same material information jointly requested, earlier than I did, by Gen. Eli Rio, Mr. Augusto Lagman and Mr. Frank Ysaac, the TnTrio.

The refusal of Comelec to release my requested information in 15 days as required by law, and credible evidence our Movement has obtained in our four-month search, indicate that there was no such transmission of 20M votes, and those 20M votes were in fact non-existent. That election was rigged!

Given such troubling circumstances, I have decided, as a concerned citizen, I must file Articles of Impeachment in Congress against the five Commissioners for culpable violation of the constitution. On March 10, 2023, I sent a final notice, attached, giving Comelec seven days to provide me and the public, that proof of transmission of the supposed 20M votes, failing in which will constrain me to file Articles of Impeachment in Congress against the five commissioners.

Another election is coming in 2025. Regardless of the outcome of the impeachment case I will file in ten days, or soon after a congressperson makes an indorsement of the Articles of Impeachment required by law, it is my intention, and my hope, that my action will spur a serious effort on the part of our decision makers to stop this vicious cycle of every election being tainted by irregularity.

I need your support in this difficult endeavor I feel I must pursue to conclusion. I will appreciate your sharing this email with as many friends as you can reach.

Thank you.

Col. Leonardo O. Odono (Ret.) PMA Class of 1964 A Filipino CTTO

....

24

THANK YOU COMELEC IT PERSONNEL FOR RESPONDING TO OUR APPEAL TO WHISTLEBLOWERS! THEY EXPOSED THE BIGGEST ELECTORAL SCAM! – Tina A. Astorga – June 13, 2023

Whoever posted the RAW FILES on the Comelec website have exposed the biggest SCAM in our election history!

Finally the expose explains the 20 million votes in 41 minutes of the first hour when the VCMs were not yet ready to transmit votes to the transparency servers. These votes were coming from Private IP addresses which were illegal local networks rather from actual VCM transmissions!

These were not Public IP addresses of Telcos through which the VCM transmit DIRECTLY to the Comelec transparency servers. This is the reason why

Comelec has not published the Telcos transmission logs because there is nothing of the 20 million votes recorded in these logs because they were transmitted by illegal private networks!

The Comelec IT personnel who exposed the SCAM deserve the nation's salute for their courage and patriotism! They are our new heroes!

Rise, Philippines, rise! The hour of reckoning has come! Either we fight for truth and justice or be victims of lie and deceit, and be ruled by an ILLEGAL gov't.

IMPEACH Comelec, FILE criminal charges against the agents of the SCAM, & OUST the ILLEGAL gov't!

....

25
TNTRIO and Johnny Memo Commented at facebook – Junw 13 2023

It could be seen as IMPOSSIBLE for the Present CONGRESS of the Philippines to be Productive because it has no Support from the Filipino People and obviously had no support from the World International Communities who had already Known the Biggest PH Election Scandals as Exposed by their Representation of Witnesses but Testimonies of their INTERNATIONAL FOREIGN ELECTION OBSERVERS who had Published their Findings that the 2019 & 2022 PH Elections were declared by them as 'MOCKED ELECTIONS' obviously masterminded by RRDuterte and his regime, which was Corroborated by PH Findings hence there is now this PH

Trending Filipino People Election Protest as headed by the TNTrio who had Filed the Case entitled the 'MANDAMUS' of which this present Syndicate Admin is all in cahoots of their evil deeds of doing 'Delaying Tactics' to Hear and Decide the 'MANDAMUS Case' which is now a 'JUSTICE DELAYED IS A JUSTICE DENIED'.

The TRUTH of the 'MANDAMUS' will be the END of this present Organized Crime Syndicate comprising of PH FRAUD Government Officials who were NOT ELECTED but Fraudulently & Unlawfully installed into their Government Positions by a Series of MOCKED ELECTIONS masterminded by the CULPRIT TRAITOR but the Killer CRIMINAL RRDuterte.

The TRUTH of the 'MANDAMUS' Will Set Free the Filipino People from Evil Rule of BBM/DUTERTE Organized Crime Syndicate of an Admin of the Government of the Philippines.

The Whole World is to Unite to PUSH for the World Peace and to RESTORE the World Morality for TRUTH JUSTICE & RIGHTEOUSNESS Hence to Expose the TRUTH of the Filipino People's Case the 'MANDAMUS'.

FAKE
PRESIDENT!

INSTALLED BY A
CRIMINAL
ORGANIZATION!

....

26
Tell it to SunStar: Mandamus and impeachment: A democratic call for government action - B Y
ALENN NIDEA
April 09, 2023

TNTrio, the group and the letter T stated twice, stand for truth and transparency.

Trio is a group of three individuals united for the purpose of executing a common act for a common purpose. The individuals are Augusto "Gus" Lagman, former commissioner-Commission on Elections (Comelec), former president-National Movement for Free Elections (Namfrel), columnist-Manila Times, "Let's Face It"; Eliseo Rio, Jr., retired brigadier general, former secretary-Department of Information and Communications Technology, former chairman-Comelec Advisory Council, Electronics and Communication; and

Franklin Ysaac, former president-Financial Executives Institute of the Philippines (Finex), owner-Franklin Financials, banking and finance technology consultancy, retired banker. They have a common purpose — to uncover the Truth and demand transparency on official governmental action (the Comelec's).

TNT is a powerful substance called "trinitrotoluene," a combination of nitroglycerine and other chemicals. TNT is commonly known as an explosive.

The chemical process that results from its ignition causes an explosion. That, in another sense, TNT can stand for Truth and Transparency is a coincidence, but appears more to be a divine confluence in meaning because the revelation of truth through transparency in one's action can ignite a most explosive event, a conflagration that may roar into a full-scale revolution that can consume the entire nation.

With that in mind, TNTrio is a most appropriate play on letters and words as it relates to what it wants to achieve.

The Trio is asking the Supreme Court (SC) of the Philippines, in a most democratic way by filing a special civil action called mandamus, to command Comelec to preserve all data records and transmission logs supporting the vote count in the May 9, 2022 Philippine national elections.

The action of mandamus in the Philippines is a transplant on Philippine law and jurisprudence. Mandamus, a Latin word meaning "we command," is a judicial writ issued by a court to an inferior tribunal, a public official, an administrative agency, a corporation, or a person demanding the performance of a specific obligatory act under the law or a statutory duty. It was first used in English courts in the 17th century and migrated to the courts in the American colonies.

Marbury v. Madison (1803) is the landmark US SC on mandamus, which established for the first time that federal courts have the power to overturn an act of

Congress on the ground that it violates the US Constitution. The Philippine judicial system is heavily influenced by US laws in resolving constitutional and legal matters. Philippine courts often cite American case law in deciding cases with similar factual elements and legal issues.

TNTrio's petition for mandamus is asking the Philippine SC to command Comelec and the telecom companies to preserve the transmission logs in connection with the May 2022 elections and for Comelec to provide digital copies to the petitioners. It was triggered by TNTrio's incredulity at the results shown in the transparency server that more than 20 million votes have been transmitted by 8:02 p.m. on May 9, 2022, one hour after the closing of the polls, and suspicion that cheating might have occurred in the counting of votes due to a constant difference of about 40 percent between the votes of the two leading presidential candidates. The main objective of TnTrio is to prevent the destruction of evidence that might be useful and crucial in future cases.

If the SC grants the mandamus petition, it will enable TNTrio, composed of information technology experts in their own rights, to determine the validity and legitimacy of the results shown in the transparency server and demonstrate to the public whether the person who was proclaimed as the supposed winner is legitimate or fake. If an examination of the transmission logs would show that no 20 million votes were transmitted by 8:02 p.m. of May 9, 2022, a big dark cloud of doubt would hang over the legitimacy of the declared president of the Philippines. The Trio is representing the entire Filipino electorate and the whole Filipino nation at large, whose daily lives are constantly affected by the acts of a declared president whose legitimacy might be in question.

The SC has ordered the Comelec and the telecom companies to comment on the TNTrio's petition for mandamus. However, Comelec failed to do so within the 10-day period given by the SC. This prompted retired Lt. Col. Leonardo Odoño to threaten to impeach the Comelec commissioners for betrayal of public trust. Unfortunately, by law, the case has to pass through the Philippine Congress. A lawmaker has to sponsor the impeachment case, have it go through approval by the House in a plenary session and transmit the articles of impeachment to the Senate for trial.

Whatever the legal formalities are, the impeachment case is a perfect follow-through for the mandamus petition of the explosive Trio. As in a motor car, mandamus is the spark that ignites the engine and impeachment is the step that accelerates the car into motion.

The movers are the TNTrio and Ret. Lt. Col. Odoño, with the help of Atty. Mel Magdamo, an IT professional and a former senior lawyer from the Comelec.

Anyone who closely followed the daily coverage of the election process would recall how the numbers came out from the counting being done by the Comelec at that time. You could see the pattern in the numbers that were coming out. Every day that you tuned in, your eyes would grow wider at each count, in disbelief over the outrageous numbers. That early, postings on social media from people who know technology expressed the same growing incredulity that you would have on the results of the counting that was taking place.

When it ended, there was no public outcry about what took place. It was disgusting. You'd feel hopeless that the general public looked resigned and calmly took the numbers that came out. And then, the proclamation and inauguration of the declared president that followed was peaceful and looked like a normal and regular event that usually follows a national election. But you couldn't stop fuming inside, and could only express disgust and helplessness with close friends who shared your belief of the fraud perpetrated on the unfortunate Filipino people.

With the twin actions of Mandamus and Impeachment, the movers want the formal action to gain traction, whip up support from the people, and ignite public protests.

That the Trio discovered each other at those critical times in the electoral results process is fortuitous. That they decided to unite as a combined force which resulted in their having filed a formal mandamus petition is divinely inspired. As things are unfolding, their discovery of each other at those crucial moments may as well be pre-ordained.

Thankfully, there are activist groups like Malaya International that exist and persist to fight. On the periphery, too, are concerned citizens who are bound by a common desire and fire to continue to help and fight. They kicked off by initiating an online forum that advocated for the pending Mandamus and Impeachment cases and provided the movers a platform to explain the issues.

(About the author: Alenn Nidea lives in New York City, NY. He is a Philippine attorney registered with the Office of Court Administration, New York State. He works as a financial professional and pursues an advocacy providing legal consulting services to the Filipino community in Queens, New York City.)

....

27
Posters

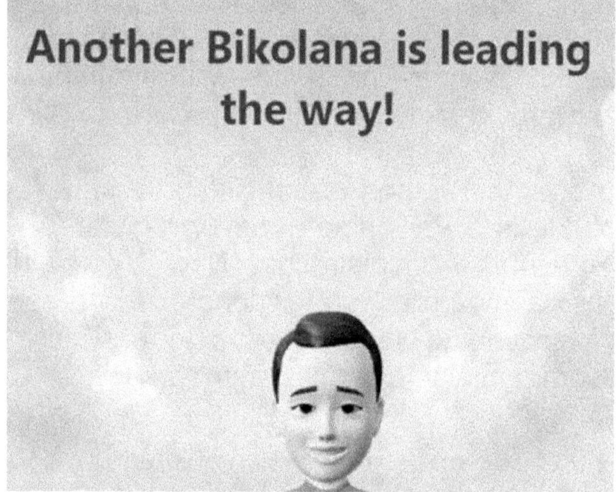

Nice to remember the kakampink crowds in 2022. It would be nicer if more of them signed the Truth Petition!

The true test of a strong leader is one who doesn't waver unless the leader wants to waive that chance!

Imprisoned for 6 years on mock up charges, she never broke down and is emerging as the next true leader!

Go spread the good news to all who are waiting to be saved! Sign up people's mandamus now so we can save ourselves!

Ano na, Comelec!

Bakit hindi ninyo ipinapaliwanag at sinusuportahan ng totoong ebidensya ang mga kadudadudang resulta na ipinahayag ninyo 'nung nakaraang eleksyon? At bakit hindi ninyo inilalabas 'yong mga 'VCM transmission logs' na hinihingi ng TNTrio? Kasabwat ba kayo sa pandaraya? Pakisagot lang.

Ipaglaban ang karapatan nating malaman ang katotohanan. Bayan 

Despite being in their late 70s,
the TNTrio continues to fight for the nation,
risking their own safety.
However, the question remains:
WHERE ARE THE FILIPINO YOUTH IN THIS FIGHT?

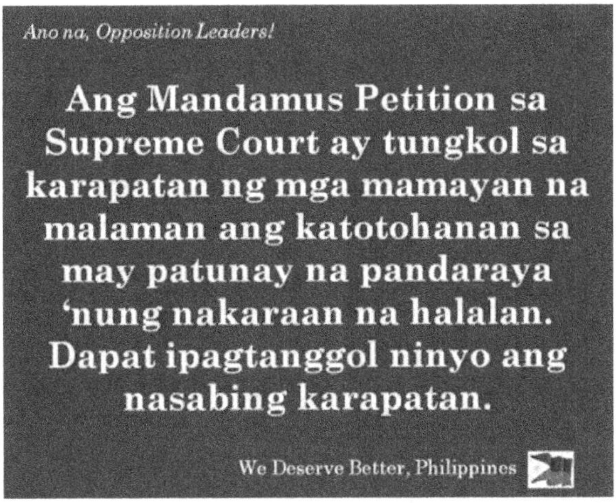

Ano na, Opposition Leaders!
Ang Mandamus Petition sa Supreme Court ay tungkol sa karapatan ng mga mamayan na malaman ang katotohanan sa may patunay na pandaraya 'nung nakaraan na halalan. Dapat ipagtanggol ninyo ang nasabing karapatan.
We Deserve Better, Philippines

When my kids asked why I haven't given up yet, I replied" This is for you, keeping our country safe from these wreckers!"

COMELEC can't show Telcos' CDRs because VCM transmissions did not pass thru telco networks in the 1st Hour. Illegal LANs were used.

Watch for the latest as our legal experts nail the loopholes in the lapses of the regulators !

Spending an hour with the best legal mind on constitutional matter is equivalent to a 4 year time in law school!

Hindi paninira ang pagsasabi ng totoo. Lalo na kung pilit kang nililinlang at nililito. Walang MAGNANAKAW na nagmamahal sa kapwa. Walang MAGNANAKAW na nagmamahal sa bansa.

TNTrio's mandamus + tens of thousands of People's Mandamus will ensure Victory for the Filipino people !

People's Mandamus thousands of signatures is People Power in the making !

There's no tomorrow if we let them get away with the election crime of the century!

TNTrio's search for Truth is done! We turn over the command to the presidential bet who was misled by her IT! Endorse mandamus

Signing the people's mandamus cannot be rigged! No fake signature and you cannot sign more than once!

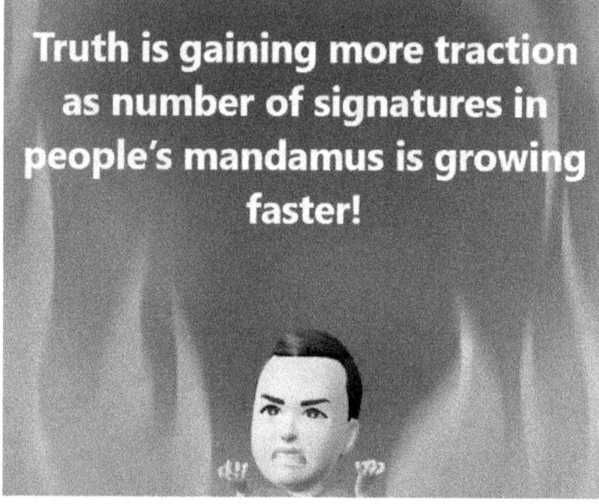

+Eliseo Rio Jr + Gus Lagman   *p98*

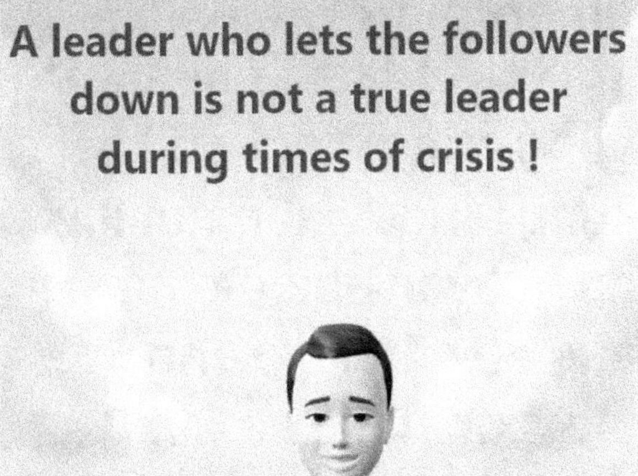

Hurry up! Sign up the people's mandamus petition now and join the thousands who will witness the people's victory!

"Importante maipakita
natin na malinis at honest
yung ating election kasi
kung hinde natin malinis
ito ngayon aba eto na
ang election type ng
election natin sa 2023...
2025... FOREVER"

— Sir Eliseo Rio Jr.

The truth train is on and we welcome growing numbers who sign up People's Mandamus and join this train!

Hindi pa tapos ang eleksyon! Make a choice-Sign the People's Mandamus or Suffer 5 more years of illegitimacy!

The truth train is on and we welcome growing numbers who sign up People's Mandamus and join this train!

The TELCOS' Call Detail Records (CDRs) would show that there were almost no VCM transmissions thru their networks in the 1st hour.

Telcos' CDRs will show that there were NO VCM transmissions to account for the 20M+ votes counted at the first hour.

Thank God for the IT experts! They have broken open the seal of the conspiracy! There is no lie that is forever hidden in the dark!

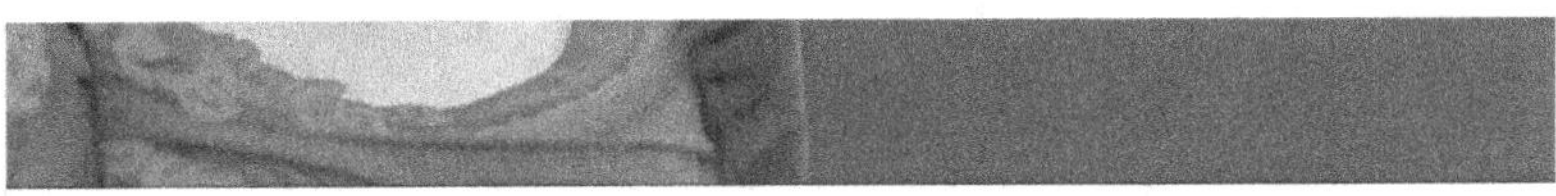

Eh Di Shing
1d · 🌐

Simply because THEY ARE NOT.

THE MAJORITY DID NOT VOTE FOR THEM. IT WAS THE WORK OF SD CARD. IN SHORT, THEY ARE FAKE.

Seems that something's happening now to the SSS pension. Lots of complaints now re non release of the pension since May! Na-Maharlika na ba?

#3
The ER data received by the Transparency Server from May 9th, 7:00 PM, to the afternoon of May 13th DOES NOT MATCH the data in the Reception Logs uploaded on COMELEC's website on March 23, 2023.

https://bit.ly/mandamuspetition

#3
Ang data na ipinakita ng natanggap na ERs ng Transparency Server mula 7:00 PM ng Mayo 9 hanggang hapon ng Mayo 13, HINDI TUMUTUGMA sa data na ipinakita sa mga Reception Logs na inilagay sa website ng COMELEC noong Marso 23, 2023.

#1
The Transparency Server (TS) received several Election Results HOURS BEFORE they were transmitted by the precinct VCMs. This suggests that whoever manipulated the TS results had prior knowledge of the "official" results even before counting began.

#2
Statistically IMPOSSIBLE data showed consistent ratios of actual voters to registered voters across multiple provinces, remaining unchanged over a two-hour period.

Countdown to more legal filings to ferret out the truth is in the offing ! We will keep you posted! Pray to Almighty to guide us!

In the "Raw Files" uploaded by COMELEC
on their website on March 23, 2022,
the following observations were made:

Within the first hour of counting by
the Transparency Server (TS),
multiple precinct Election Returns (ERs)
received from DIFFERENT VCMs
HAD THE SAME IP ADDRESS.
This indicates that the TS
was counting votes faster than
the VCMs were transmitting,
indicating that the ERs originated
from ONE FABRICATED SOURCE.

The Good Lord answered our
prayers! He gave us tough IT
and Legal Experts!Miracles
still happen! Thank you Lord!

From day one, our Lord
tested our patience as He
guided us during our truth
travails!Thank you Lord and
all our supporters!

Even after we have uncovered the truth, the lackadaisical attention turning even to malaise will not deter us!

The Good Lord answered our prayers! He gave us tough IT and Legal Experts!Miracles still happen! Thank you Lord!

This is the enigma that Filipinos suffer from after every election! This has to change unless we accept all the lies about election!

We thank everyone who offered prayers to our endeavor as we pursue case after case to pin them down!

The legal pundit warns that if the SC dismisses our case which is a constitutional issue, then we have a crisis!

Tina A. Astorga
2h

Dear VP Leni:
The call of mission is so compelling, one can never live with a no. The lines have been drawn. To say no is the death of hope.

The evidence is based on hard facts and not on hearsay!

12M votes
were officially transmitted by the VCMs
NOW IT IS FRAUDULENT THAT THE TRANSPARENCY SERVER WILL SHOW A COUNT OF 20M+ VOTES AT 8:02PM WHEN THE OFFICIALLY TRANSMITTED VOTES AT 8:02PM IS ONLY 12M+ VOTES. WHERE DID THE ADDITIONAL 8M+ VOTES COME FROM?
- General Eliseo Rio, Jr (R)
TRANSPARENCY SERVER
20M

Yes, truth warriors!
Miracles still happen
when we pray as one
and we are united in
our petition. Amen.

The moment of truth is
now at hand! The
momentum is growing as
our prayers have been
heard and a revelation is
about to unfold.

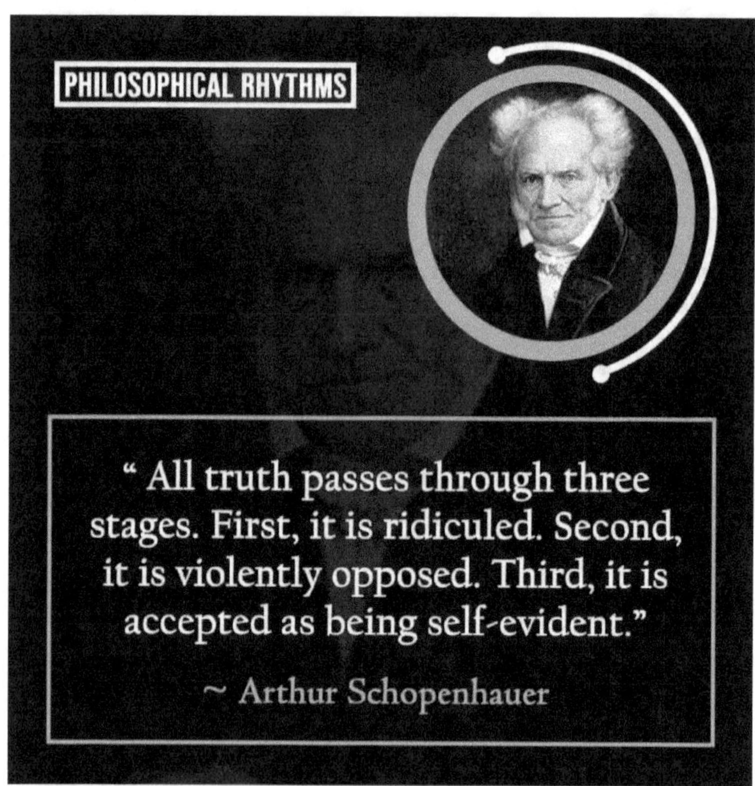
PHILOSOPHICAL RHYTHMS
" All truth passes through three stages. First, it is ridiculed. Second, it is violently opposed. Third, it is accepted as being self-evident."
~ Arthur Schopenhauer

Truth and Transparency Trio
PH ELECTION 2022: MANIPULATED
TRUTH
NOT FOR SALE

www.ingramcontent.com/pod-product-compliance
Lightning Source LLC
Chambersburg PA
CBHW051754250726
48659CB00001B/404